PASS Cambridge BEC Higher

An examination preparation course

Updated for the revised exam

WORKBOOK

with Answer Key

Ian Wood

HEINLE
CENGAGE Learning™

Summertown
Publishing

Australia • Brazil • Japan • Korea • Mexico • Singapore • Spain • United Kingdom • United States

PASS Cambridge BEC Higher Workbook
Ian Wood

Publisher: Nick Sheard

Production Controller: Tom Relf

Head of Inventory: Jane Glendening

Cover design: Richard Morris, Stonesfield Design

ISBN: 978-1-902741-39-0

Heinle, Cengage Learning EMEA
Cheriton House, North Way, Andover, Hampshire, SP10 5BE, United Kingdom

Cengage Learning is a leading provider of customised learning solutions with office locations around the globe, including Singapore, the United Kingdom, Australia, Mexico, Brazil and Japan. Locate our local office at: **international.cengage.com/region**

Cengage Learning products are represented in Canada by Nelson Education Ltd.

Visit Heinle online at **elt.heinle.com**
Visit our corporate website at **cengage.com**

MIX
Paper from
responsible sources
FSC® C013604

Printed in the United Kingdom by Antony Rowe
8 9 10 – 12

PASS
Cambridge
BEC Higher

An examination preparation course
Updated for the revised exam

WORKBOOK
with Answer key

Ian Wood

Summertown
Publishing

Introduction

The Cambridge Business English Certificate

The Cambridge Business English Certificate (BEC) is an international Business English examination which offers a language qualification for learners who use, or will need to use, English for their work. It is available at three levels.

Level 1 Preliminary
Level 2 Vantage
Level 3 Higher

Cambridge BEC is a practical examination that focuses on English in business-related situations. The emphasis is on the development of language skills for work: reading, writing, listening and speaking.

Pass Cambridge BEC Higher

As an examination preparation course, *Pass Cambridge BEC Higher* focuses on all the language skills tested at BEC Higher (reading, writing, listening and speaking) as well as the examination skills required to fully prepare students who wish to take the exam.

Pass Cambridge BEC Higher Workbook

As an important component of the *Pass Cambridge BEC Higher* course, the Workbook is a language-focused supplement to the Coursebook. Each unit is split into a grammar, reading, vocabulary and writing section.

Pass Cambridge BEC Higher Workbook includes the following features.

- **Grammar**

   Each grammar section begins with a clear and full explanation of the grammar presented in the Coursebook. This is followed by practice exercises that test and develop students' knowledge. A full Answer key is provided at the back of the book.

- **Reading**

   Each reading section begins with a text that complements or extends the corresponding course-book topic and is similar to texts in the BEC Higher reading examination. The text is followed by exercises that practise various reading skills.

- **Vocabulary / Writing**

   Each vocabulary section recycles key items from the *Pass Cambridge BEC Higher* Coursebook and is followed by a writing exercise that provides practice in writing emails, formal letters, faxes and brief exam-style reports. A full Answer key is provided at the back of the book.

- **Review**

   There are two language reviews in *Pass Cambridge BEC Higher* Workbook: after Units 4 and 8. Each review consists of one hundred grammar questions, which revise the grammar of the previous four units, and fifty multiple-choice vocabulary questions also based on the previous four units. A full Answer key is provided at the back of the book.

Pass BEC Higher Workbook

Organisation

Present simple and continuous

The present simple is used in the following ways.

- to describe facts and permanent situations
  We **don't have** a large hierarchy.

- to describe routines and fixed timetables
  Our managers **report** in on a daily basis.
  The train to Bucharest **leaves** at six thirty tomorrow.

The present continuous is used in the following ways.

- to describe unfinished or temporary actions or situations
  We**'re restructuring** the department at the moment.
  I**'m working** in another department for a few weeks.

- to describe future arrangements
  When **are** you **holding** the teamwork seminar?

Note! We do not use the present continuous to express the following.

routines (usually, normally etc.)	emotions (like, love, hate)
ownership (own, have, need)	opinions (think, believe, feel)
senses (see, hear, feel)	

Past simple

The past simple is used in the following ways.

- to describe finished events
  I **sent** the report to the client yesterday.

- to refer to definite or finished time (ago, yesterday, last, all dates)
  The meeting **didn't finish** until 3 o'clock.

Present perfect

The present perfect is used in the following ways.

- to describe events that started in the past and are still continuing
  Some employees **have been working** from home since 1998.

- to refer to unfinished time (already, today, this, for, since, yet, ever, never)
  Their technical support **has improved** a lot already.

- to describe changes that affect the present situation
  We**'ve just implemented** a 24-hour IT support service.

Note! The present perfect simple emphasises the product of an action while the present perfect continuous emphasises the process itself.

We**'ve reduced** our overheads by 15 per cent.
We**'ve been looking** at ways of reducing our overheads.

For expresses the duration of an action. *Since* states a starting point.

We've been working with them **for 5 years / since 1997**.

Grammar practice

Present simple and continuous **❶** Complete the sentences with the correct form of the verbs in brackets.

1 We (try) ___'re trying___ to cut costs by 20 per cent this year.
2 The post (not / arrive) _____ until 10.30.
3 How long (you / stay) _____ in Paris after the conference?
4 At the moment, I (feel) _____ we should cancel the project.
5 Who (you / report) _____ to?
6 With our teleworking initiative, we (not / need) _____ as much office space.
7 The videoconference (not / start) _____ until 3.30 this afternoon.
8 I (see) _____ the MD on Monday about working from home.

Past simple and present perfect **❷** Complete the dialogue with the correct form of the verbs in brackets.

Ingrid   Ah, Freddie, I (¹want) _____wanted_____ to talk to you about a follow-up report to that team leadership seminar we (²run) _____ last year. The MD (³ask) _____ about it the other day and wants some kind of feedback – you know, whether we (⁴do) _____ anything about the recommendations yet. That kind of thing.

Freddie   Well, we still (⁵not / implement) _____ all the recommendations as the report only (⁶come) _____ back six months ago.

Ingrid   I know. And I think that's exactly why the MD wants some kind of update. What (⁷we / do) _____ so far?

Freddie   We (⁸start) _____ screening all managerial applicants for appropriate leadership attributes but we (⁹not / manage) _____ to set up the assessment centres yet for existing team leaders.

Ingrid   And why's that?

Freddie   We (¹⁰have) _____ a few problems setting them up.

Ingrid   What kind of problems?

Freddie   Well, there (¹¹be) _____ some resistance amongst some of the managers. They think the assessments are a threat to their jobs.

Ingrid   But (¹²not / you / explain) _____ to them their jobs are safe?

Freddie   I did. But there's also the issue of who actually does the assessments.

Ingrid   Isn't that for HR to decide?

Freddie   We originally (¹³ask) _____ them to propose a framework for doing the assessments but they (¹⁴come) _____ back and said the department heads should do it as they know the managers better.

Ingrid   (¹⁵you / speak) _____ to any department heads yet?

Freddie   Yes, we (¹⁶speak) _____ to most of them last week. They (¹⁷say) _____ it would mean more unnecessary paperwork and it (¹⁸will) _____ affect their relationships with their managers.

Present perfect simple and continuous **❸** Complete the sentences with the more appropriate form of the present perfect simple or continuous.

1 We've finally finished / been finishing the company restructuring.
2 I haven't read / been reading the report yet.
3 We've run / been running training days this summer and they're proving very useful.
4 Have you filled / been filling in the questionnaire yet?
5 Staff who have worked / been working at home recently have increased productivity.
6 How long have you waited / been waiting for them to finish the report?
7 Sales have gone / been going up by 12 per cent this year.
8 Staff have worked / been working very long hours recently so they're tired.

Reading practice

1 Read the text and put the paragraphs in the correct order.

a

What happened to the teleworking revolution?

*As the new millennium approached, we all dreamt of working from the comfort of our own homes. **Tricia Patel** finds out whether reality lived up to the hype.*

It was said to be the biggest change in our working lives since the industrial revolution. New technology would make office space a thing of the past as companies would save fortunes in rent by setting employees up to work from their own homes. Employees, in turn, looked forward to a working life that started when they stumbled out of bed and sat down at their computers. Spared the stress of the daily commute, the new flexibility would finally put them in charge of their lives. The dream was an ideal win-win situation. But has reality lived up to the hype? The government recently commissioned a study to find out whether the office exodus is still continuing or whether the good old desk is once more back in fashion.

b
This definition of working from home includes people who use their own living space as part of their full-time job. This includes more mobile workers who travel a lot using their own home as a base and people who work from home at least one day a week. Seven out of ten teleworkers are likely to be men. One in four of them is employed by a company in either the business or financial services sector.

c
'The way to get around these problems is to work from home just a couple of days a week,' argues Hunt. 'That's definitely the way forward. It has all the advantages but avoids any of the downsides of teleworking. If you look at the figures, it's definitely the future.'

d
However, business change expert Marsha Hunt thinks this is not the main saving. 'The single greatest cost to an employer is recruiting and training a new employee. And with an ageing UK workforce, it's vital that companies retain staff. Giving employees the flexibility to work from home can be the difference between retaining and losing key personnel.'

e
The advantages teleworking offers these businesses have not changed. BT, who has been promoting working from home initiatives since 1992, claims to have saved £180m of office space expenditure to date. The company currently has nearly 10,000 home-based staff and with average costs per desk in the UK between £10–16,000, the attractions are obvious.

f
Further disadvantages for teleworkers include the lack of quick technical support when computers go wrong and the resentment of colleagues unhappy at not being allowed to telework themselves. However, the biggest complaint is isolation from daily office life. Many teleworkers feel cut off socially and politically from their office-based colleagues.

g
Hunt points out, though, that any employee using their own home as office space has the disadvantage of effectively subsidising the company. 'Take someone working from home in London, for example. Office space is massively expensive in London, so if the company can put desks in people's homes, the employees are effectively paying to work for the company.'

h
The government Labour Force study shows that the number of people now working from home has risen to 1.5 million, or approximately 6 per cent of the UK workforce. The figures represent an increase of 19 per cent on the previous year, so in terms of numbers alone, teleworking is indeed more popular than ever before. The study also profiles who is most likely to work from home and an explanation of exactly what counts as working from home.

2 **Match a summary with each paragraph of the text.**

1 introduction   *a*
2 figures to show teleworking trends
3 details on how the figures were arrived at
4 the advantages for companies
5 the main advantage for companies
6 a disadvantage for employees
7 further disadvantages for employees
8 conclusion

3 **Read the text again and choose the correct option for each question.**

1 The Labour Force study revealed that

   a) about 6 per cent of the UK workforce works at home.
   b) 1.5 million more people in the UK now work from home.
   c) 19 per cent of the UK workforce now works at home.

2 The definition of working from home does not include

   a) sales reps who spend most of their time travelling.
   b) people who only work from home one or two days a week.
   c) people working at home in part-time jobs.

3 According to Marsha Hunt, the main savings teleworking offers companies are in

   a) rent for office space.
   b) equipment and technical support.
   c) recruitment and training.

4 Teleworkers subsidise companies by

   a) providing free office space.
   b) doing unpaid overtime.
   c) reducing staff turnover.

5 The main problem facing teleworkers is

   a) the lack of technical support.
   b) not being part of everyday office life.
   c) the jealousy of office-based colleagues.

6 Marsha Hunt thinks that in future

   a) the trend towards working from home will decrease.
   b) more people will work from home one or two days a week.
   c) companies will continue to reduce office space.

Vocabulary **4** **Match the words from the text with their definitions.**

1 hype   a) disadvantage
2 commute   b) publicity that exaggerates the importance of something
3 exodus   c) bitterness or anger at someone or something
4 downside   d) being kept away from other people and things
5 isolation   e) daily journey to work
6 resentment   f) departure of many people at the same time

Vocabulary practice

Managing ❶ Use the noun form of the following verbs to complete the email below.

> ~~brief~~   collaborate   respond   co-ordinate
> motivate   assign   assess   balance   allocate

RE: New sales project

From: Higgins, Alan [ajh@concam.co.uk]

Sent: Friday 7 December 10.17pm
To: Brownjohn, Cornelia
Subject: RE: New sales project

Connie

Sorry you couldn't make it to the meeting yesterday. I've attached your project ¹____*brief*____ outlining the strategy for the new sales project. It's going to be a tough ²_____ with ambitious targets but I'm sure you can do it.

We've already started recruiting the new team and the ³_____ has been great. I'll hand over all the CVs for your ⁴_____. I think it's very important that we get the right ⁵_____ of personalities within the team - we don't want compatibility problems that will have a negative effect on ⁶_____. I think it's vital you concentrate on team ⁷_____ - so don't get too 'hands on' and involved on a day-to-day basis. The budget ⁸_____ is quite generous so you should be able to afford to recruit the right people.

And finally, don't forget that ⁹_____ with other offices is one of the prime objectives - so make sure communication channels are set up properly right at the start.

Good luck!

---

❷ Match the words then use them to complete the sentences below.

real-time	units
online	information
flexible	advantage
business	support
competitive	working
communication	structure
company	processes
operating	channels

1   Technology now gives us *real-time information* on sales as they happen so we can order products the moment we look as if we might run out of stock.

2   The company is divided into six separate _____ .

3   We're assessing the effectiveness of our _____ to see whether we can improve the flow of information between project team members.

4 They've streamlined their _____ by removing some of the layers of hierarchy in senior management.

5 I don't think the new _____ policies have increased productivity, but letting employees work from home has certainly improved morale.

6 Our web team will provide the _____ for the new product.

7 We're hoping that by producing in the Czech Republic, we can get good quality at good prices, which will give us a _____ over our rivals.

8 She wants us to review our _____ to find out how we can reduce production times and waste levels.

Describing tasks ❸ **Match the words with opposite meanings.**

1	nimble	a)	dynamic
2	static	b)	hampered
3	feasible	c)	focused
4	flexible	d)	simple
5	complex	e)	rigid
6	diverse	f)	impossible

Writing practice: Organising a report

Formal report ❶ You have been asked to write a report on how communication could be improved within your project team. You have made the following notes to help you plan your report. Use the notes to write a report of 200–250 words.

Notes on planning a report
Report making recommendations

- Start with an introduction
  aim - to identify problems with communication within the team & make recommendations how to improve it

- Findings - state your main points & give one or more supporting ideas for each main point
  1) whole team rarely gets together
  2) people in different departments are in different parts of the building
  3) people don't copy emails to other team members

  - Conclusion - summarise your main points
    1) improving procedures will improve attitudes among team members
    2) no real reason why communication shouldn't be better

  - Recommendation - say what action needs to be taken
    1) schedule weekly meetings
    2) ensure people are copied in on emails
    3) organise a team-building seminar

  Don't forget to lay it out in separate paragraphs with headings!!

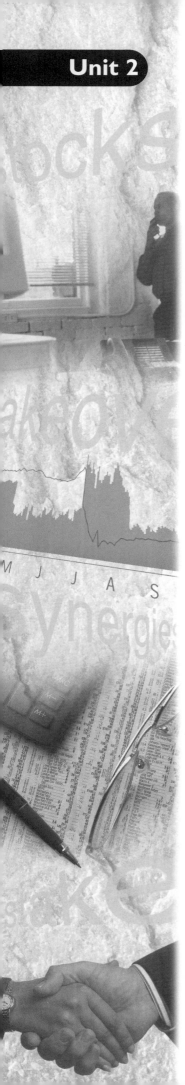

Mergers

Relative clauses

Defining clauses define a noun and have the following forms.

- with *who, which* or *that* (no commas)
  *The news will affect all the companies **which / that** do business with them.*

- without a relative pronoun (if it is the object of the verb in the clause)
  *They've renamed the company **(that)** they bought last year.*

- with *whom* (to refer to the object of the clause – formal style only)
  *The new CEO **whom** they have hired has a marvellous reputation.*

- with *whose* (to show possession)
  *They merged with a company **whose** products complemented their own.*

Non-defining clauses give extra information and have the following forms.

- with *who, which, whom* or *whose* (extra information within commas)
  *The deal, **which** is worth £600m, will be completed tomorrow.*

Note!   *That* is used only in defining relative clauses.

The offer price, ~~that~~ was confirmed yesterday, will surely attract investors.
*The offer price, **which** was confirmed yesterday, will surely attract investors.*

In very formal style, *whom* is necessary following a preposition.

*I would like to thank Jo Cox, without **whom** the deal couldn't have succeeded.*

Adjectives and adverbs

Adjectives are used in the following ways.

- before nouns
  *There's been a **dramatic** rise in the price of oil this week.*

- after the verbs *be, become, seem, appear, look, feel, remain*
  *The forthcoming merger looks **interesting**.*

- in comparatives and superlatives
  *Our stock market performance wasn't **as strong as** last year.*
  *Vodafone is the world's **largest** mobile telecoms group.*

Adverbs are used in the following ways.

- after verbs
  *They expanded **quickly** in the late 1990s.*

- before adjectives and other adverbs
  *Many companies are struggling in **increasingly** competitive markets.*
  *The service sector did **extremely** well this year.*

- in comparatives
  *Their share price has risen **more sharply** than their rival's.*

Note!   Some adverbs have irregular forms.

fast - fast   good - well   hard - hard   late - late

Grammar practice

Relative pronouns ❶ Join the sentences using an appropriate relative pronoun where necessary.

1 They'll need to negotiate with the unions. The unions are afraid of job cuts.
  They'll need to negotiate with the unions, who are afraid of job cuts.

2 The offer price is $18 a share. It was confirmed yesterday.
  _____

3 They've increased the offer. They made the original offer last week.
  _____

4 The merger will make them the biggest bank in the UK. It hasn't been approved yet.
  _____

5 They'll need the approval of private shareholders. They own 35% of the company.
  _____

6 Shareholders have lost faith in the board. Its expansion strategy has lost £800m.
  _____

7 The merger was masterminded by Luc Van der Saar. All credit should go to him.
  _____

8 The company sold the web TV subsidiary. The company bought it two years ago.
  _____

9 After the merger they closed 64 retail outlets. The outlets were in similar locations.
  _____

10 We're having problems integrating two management styles. They are very different.
  _____

Adjectives and adverbs ❷ Complete the report with the correct form of the words in brackets.

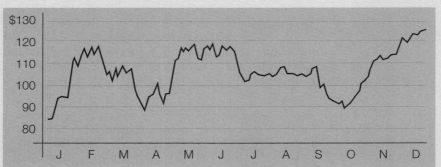

IBM share price performance 2001

The IBM share price began 2001 with a (¹*dramatic*) ___*dramatic*___ rise, soaring from $85 to over $110. In February prices became (²*erratic*) _____, fluctuating between $110 and $120, before then dropping (³*sudden*) _____ to back below $90 by April. The share price soon rose (⁴*quick*) _____ again to over $110 by May. Throughout May and June there were further (⁵*marked*) _____ fluctuations between $110 and $120. By July, however, the price had slid again (⁶*slight*) _____ back to just over $100. Over the next three months the price remained (⁷*reasonable*) _____ (⁸*stable*) _____ around the $105 mark. However, the price then fell (⁹*sharp*) _____ once more back to the $90 level in October. There then followed a (¹⁰*strong*) _____ recovery with shares climbing (¹¹*steady*) _____ until the end of the year, ending with a 52-week high of $125.

Reading practice

1 Read the text and choose the most suitable headline from the following options.

   a) Media giants caught in hostile takeover bid
   b) AOL announces joint venture with Time Warner
   c) Old media meets new internet
   d) Time Warner seals distribution deal with AOL

Media giants announce world's largest merger in attempt to marry the value of traditional assets with the new potential of internet growth.

Internet services giant America Online (AOL) today announced it intends to merge with media conglomerate Time Warner. With AOL having a current market capitalisation of $163bn and Time Warner currently valued at $83bn, the companies announced that the $350bn all stock merger would be the largest in the world. AOL will take a majority stake in the new group, with its shareholders owning 55 per cent. Both boards unanimously approved the deal and AOL's Steve Case will be Chairman. Reaction to the announcement has been very positive, with share prices rising sharply on the news. At the end of trading, AOL finished 19 per cent up, with Time Warner shares also increasing 12 per cent.

Clicks and mortar

The merger signals the first attempt to merge the potential of internet growth with the old world assets of a traditional company in a so-called 'clicks-and-mortar' model. Many internet companies enjoy huge stock market capitalisation despite low revenues and few tangible assets. Many traditional companies, on the other hand, have sound revenue models and large assets but lack the expertise and skills to take advantage of internet growth. Although AOL has vast online experience, reliable distribution and a massive market share, it has no content. Time Warner's content is its strength, especially in the vital area of news. One of the world's largest media companies, Time Warner owns leading cable news channels CNN and TNT as well as entertainment channels such as Cartoon Network and a host of magazines and other publications. What Time Warner lacked, however, was a way of delivering this content over the internet. With the merger, Time Warner can now push this through AOL's internet gateway while AOL will be able to promote its services through TV screens across the US.

Going it alone

Both partners had been trying for some time to independently achieve what the combined group promises to do. Founded in 1995, AOL has been a leading provider of interactive services and net technologies and is one of the very few firms to make a successful internet-based business model; theirs currently has 20 million subscribers. Major acquisitions of rival CompuServe and leading internet company Netscape have strengthened the core business but done little to solve the lack of content. Time Warner, meanwhile, has poured millions into unsuccessful internet ventures that suffered from a lack of experience and strategy disagreements. However, the purchase of CNN gave it one of the world's leading news websites as well as bringing in the skills and expertise that had taken CNN Interactive into profitability.

Difficulties

Although the merger appears to offer both companies solutions to their needs, it will not be without its risks. The confidence in internet stocks that created AOL's massive market capitalisation so suddenly could disappear just as quickly in the future. The move will also come under regulatory review and protest from rivals such as Disney-owned ABC. Even if these obstacles are cleared, there are no guarantees that such a large company will have the agility to fully exploit the rapidly-changing online environment. Moreover, any success would certainly lead to similar consolidation within the media industry and the creation of equally-powerful competitors.

❷ Read the text again and answer the questions.

1 Which of the two companies has the higher stock market valuation?
2 Which company has the most tangible assets?
3 Which company will control the newly-merged group?
4 What effect did the news have on AOL's and Time Warner's share prices?
5 Why was AOL interested in Time Warner?
6 What did AOL have to offer?
7 Why did AOL buy CompuServe and Netscape?
8 Why were Time Warner's internet ventures unsuccessful?
9 What did the purchase of CNN offer Time Warner?
10 What could stop the merger happening?

❸ Match the figures with what they refer to in the text.

1 163 billion
2 55 per cent
3 20 million
4 19 per cent
5 350 billion

a) increase in AOL's share price
b) market capitalisation of AOL
c) AOL shareholders' stake in the new company
d) number of AOL subscribers
e) value of the newly-merged AOL Time Warner

❹ What are the relationships between the following companies?

1 AOL / CompuServe   *AOL owns CompuServe* ....
2 CNN / TNT   ....
3 Time Warner / Cartoon Network   ....
4 AOL / Netscape   ....
5 Disney / ABC   ....
6 AOL Time Warner / Disney   ....

Vocabulary **❺** Match the words with their definitions.

1 gateway
2 stock
3 market capitalisation
4 tangible assets
5 revenue
6 conglomerate
7 subscriber
8 regulatory review
9 agility
10 consolidation

a) large company consisting of many smaller companies
b) distribution channel on the internet
c) person who pays for a service on a regular basis
d) ability to move quickly in different directions
e) government check to ensure fair competition
f) total value of all of a company's shares
g) streamlining of an industry by takeovers or mergers
h) objects owned by a company
i) shares in a company
j) income

❻ Complete the sentences with the following words.

| although   however   ~~despite~~   while   as well as |

1 AOL is highly-valued ___*despite*___ having very few concrete assets.
2 _____ Time Warner has content, it doesn't have a way of delivering it online.
3 AOL will get content _____ Time Warner can distribute its content online.
4 Time Warner owns CNN _____ many other cable channels.
5 AOL has over 20 million subscribers. What it doesn't have, _____, is good quality content to distribute to these subscribers.

Vocabulary practice

Change ❶ Match the words and phrases on the left with the more idiomatic equivalents on the right. Then match the pairs with the graphs below.

plummet ———— soar
slide ———— collapse
reach a high   fluctuate
cooling of enthusiasm   fall off
rollercoaster ride   peak
go through the roof   fall steadily

1) *collapse*
   plummet

2) _____
   _____

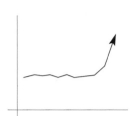

3) _____
   _____

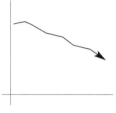

4) _____
   _____

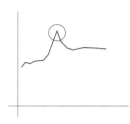

5) _____
   _____

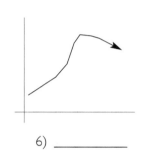

6) _____
   _____

Mergers ❷ Match the words with the definitions.

1 flotation   a) group of companies that form an alliance
2 consolidation   b) sale of shares to the public by a private company
3 dividend   c) ownership of a block of shares in a company
4 streamlining   d) merger involving only the exchange of company shares
5 synergy   e) reduction in companies in a sector through mergers
6 equity stake   f) advantage achieved by combining ideas or resources
7 stock swap   g) increase in efficiency often resulting in cost savings
8 consortium   h) annual payment made to shareholders

Odd one out ❸ Which word is the odd one out?

1 global   worldwide   international   domestic
2 joint venture   demerger   alliance   association
3 sell-off   plummet   collapse   dip
4 savings   dividends   synergies   efficiencies
5 diversify   focus   concentrate   streamline
6 acquire   take over   merge   buy

4 Do the following words refer to the advantages of a merger or possible problems? Use the words to complete the sentences below.

> integration of cultures   efficiencies   economies of scale
> destabilisation   synergies   duplicated functions
> diversification   redundancies   increased revenue

advantages	problems / disadvantages
efficiencies	*integration of cultures*

1 We achieved substantial ___efficiencies___ by cutting our costs in marketing.
2 Although we're a heavy engineering company, the acquisition of Omnitech, our hi-tech subsidiary, means _____ into new markets and sectors is now possible.
3 The very different management styles of the two companies has meant that the _____ has been particularly difficult.
4 Since the merger, we've benefited from increased know-how and _____ – particularly in the sales and marketing functions, where we've been far more effective.
5 The unions are against the merger as they think it'll lead to a lot of _____ .
6 Due to the size of the newly-merged company, we're able to negotiate better prices from suppliers and benefit from other similar _____ .
7 The _____ on this year's consolidated balance sheet is due to the recent acquisition of Incom Trading and the profits this company brought into the group.
8 The companies were very similar and the merger resulted in many _____ such as marketing and customer service - so some jobs had to go.
9 The merger rumours generated _____ within the company as several top managers left and the share price fell dramatically.

Writing practice: Describing graphs

Short report **1** You have been asked to compare your company's sales figures with the previous year. Use the graph and handwritten notes to write a short report of 120–140 words.

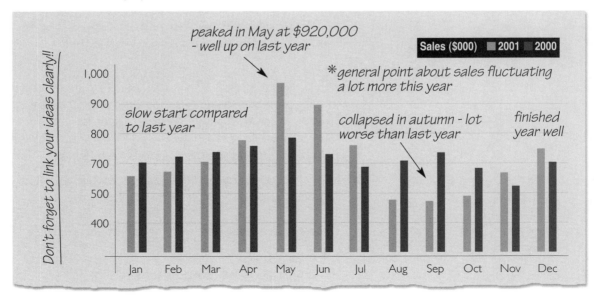

Selling

Time clauses

Present verbs are used to refer to future time after the following words: *before, after, when, as soon as, until, while.*

*You'll need to do a lot of preparation **before** you **go** to Bangladesh.*
*I'll send you a copy of the contract **as soon as** I **get** it.*

Note! The present perfect is used to emphasise that one action is complete before another one starts.

*We can't plan the stand **until** they**'ve confirmed** its location.*

The continuous is used to refer to actions in progress in the future.

*I can do some sightseeing **while** you**'re inspecting** the factory.*

Articles

The indefinite article (*a / an*) is used in the following ways.

- to refer to general singular countable nouns
  *There's **an exhibition** of office furniture in Milan this week.*

- to refer to jobs
  *She's **an export sales manager.***

- to refer to frequency
  *I go out to Russia three or **four times a year**.*

The definite article (*the*) is used in the following ways.

- to refer to nouns already mentioned or defined
  *We've got a new agent. **The** last **one** didn't promote our products enough.*

- to refer to nouns that are unique
  *We heard the news on **the radio**.*

- to refer to superlatives
  *Japan is one of **the largest** telecoms markets in the world.*

- to refer to adjectives that describe a group
  *They've been doing a lot of business with **the French**.*

No article (Ø) is used in the following situations.

- to refer to proper names (companies, sectors, cities, countries)
  *I worked in **construction** for three years in **India.***
  (But *the* is used in *The United States, The Republic of China* etc.)
  *We set up a production facility in **the Czech Republic**.*

- to refer to general uncountable or general plural nouns
  *All **trade literature** should be in the local language.*

Note! If an adjective is used before a general noun, no article is required.

*We're looking to develop **sales**.*
*We're looking to develop **overseas sales**.*

Grammar practice

Time clauses ❶ Use the following words to complete the sentences below.

| before   after   when   as soon as   until   while |

1 I'll be waiting for you at the airport ____*when*____ you arrive.
2 We'll have something to eat _____ we've seen the next client.
3 I'll do some work back at the office _____ you're meeting the next customer.
4 We can't book the hotel _____ the flights have been confirmed.
5 You'd better do some research _____ you go out there on business.
6 I'll email you the report _____ it's finished.

❷ Complete the sentences with an appropriate form of the verbs in brackets.

1 I (give) ____*'ll give*____ you a call as soon as I (get) ____*get*____ off the plane.
2 I (read) _____ the report while I (wait) _____ in the departure lounge.
3 (not / forget) _____ to write a report when you (get) _____ back home.
4 After we (finish) _____ this meeting, we (take) _____ a taxi to the hotel.
5 I (not / arrange) _____ any meetings until you (confirm) _____ the dates.
6 We (give) _____ you a call just before we (leave) _____ my hotel room.
7 I (play) _____ a bit of golf while I (visit) _____ Spain on business.
8 She (pick) _____ you up from the hotel after you (have) _____ breakfast.

Articles ❸ Complete the email with *a, an, the* or no article (Ø).

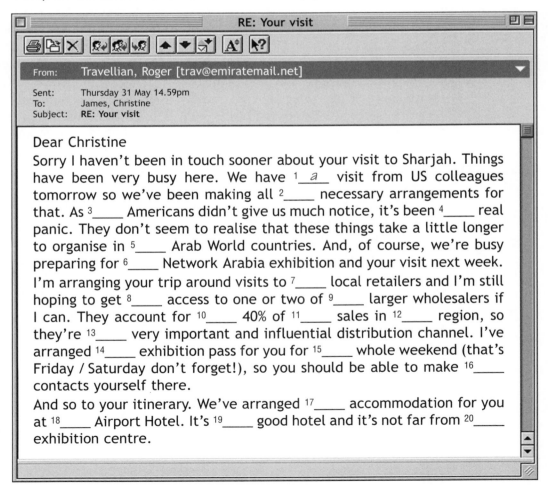

| | RE: Your visit | |

| From: | Travellian, Roger [trav@emiratemail.net] |

Sent: Thursday 31 May 14.59pm
To: James, Christine
Subject: RE: Your visit

Dear Christine

Sorry I haven't been in touch sooner about your visit to Sharjah. Things have been very busy here. We have ¹_*a*_ visit from US colleagues tomorrow so we've been making all ²____ necessary arrangements for that. As ³____ Americans didn't give us much notice, it's been ⁴____ real panic. They don't seem to realise that these things take a little longer to organise in ⁵____ Arab World countries. And, of course, we're busy preparing for ⁶____ Network Arabia exhibition and your visit next week. I'm arranging your trip around visits to ⁷____ local retailers and I'm still hoping to get ⁸____ access to one or two of ⁹____ larger wholesalers if I can. They account for ¹⁰____ 40% of ¹¹____ sales in ¹²____ region, so they're ¹³____ very important and influential distribution channel. I've arranged ¹⁴____ exhibition pass for you for ¹⁵____ whole weekend (that's Friday / Saturday don't forget!), so you should be able to make ¹⁶____ contacts yourself there.

And so to your itinerary. We've arranged ¹⁷____ accommodation for you at ¹⁸____ Airport Hotel. It's ¹⁹____ good hotel and it's not far from ²⁰____ exhibition centre.

Reading practice

1 Where do you think the article below is from?

   a) in-flight magazine
   b) company brochure
   c) business newspaper
   d) company newsletter

KINGFISHER CONTINUES GROWTH STRATEGY IN ASIA-PACIFIC

Europe's largest home improvement retailer opens Shanghai megastore reports Gillian Woo.

Kingfisher, Europe's leading home improvement retailer, continued its Asia-Pacific expansion strategy with the opening of its newest megastore in Shanghai, China. Like its other three stores in China, the Yangpu megastore will trade under its B&Q brand, the largest home improvement brand in the UK.

With over 550 home improvement stores worldwide, Kingfisher also enjoys market leadership in France, where it trades mainly under its Castorama brand, and Turkey, with its five Koçtas stores. Furthermore, it is one of Poland's largest names, with its 29 NOMI outlets. Kingfisher is also one of Europe's leading electrical retailers with its Paris-based Kingfisher Electricals operating over 800 stores in nine countries.

With such an established market position in its European homelands, Kingfisher is now looking towards the Asia-Pacific region for future growth. The company first entered China in 1995, followed a year later by the first of its ten B&Q stores in Taiwan. Sales in the area are now increasing at between 25 and 30 per cent a year and the retail giant is planning to have 58 stores operating in the region by 2005. The Yangpu megastore is the fourth of these and the largest yet. At 18,000 square feet, it is twice the size of the average UK B&Q Supercentre or Warehouse and is the same size as two football pitches. This growth is due to the increasing enthusiasm for 'Do-It-Yourself' (DIY) in China. The home improvement market was worth $22bn last year, up from $6bn two years ago. Rising living standards are enabling more and more urban Chinese to improve their modest apartments.

Moreover, Shanghai is experiencing a large construction boom with extensive government programmes rapidly pulling down inner-city slums and building new suburbs. Many of the new apartments being built are sold as empty shells with no interior walls or doors, obliging new owners to supply these along with all kitchen and bathroom fittings. The new Yangpu outlet has specially designed escalators to help customers carry such heavy purchases around the two-storey megastore.

B&Q has had to adapt to the local needs and its Shanghai store operates differently from those in the UK. Garden centres, a key feature in the UK, play no part in the Chinese format. With space being at such a premium in cities like Shanghai, most Chinese live in small apartments without a garden. Other product lines, such as soft furnishings, kitchens and bathroom fittings are just as important in China as in Europe. Wallpaper, however, does not appear in the Chinese stores due to the humid climate.

2 Read the text again and answer the questions.

1   What kind of company is Kingfisher?
2   Why is it targeting the Asia-Pacific region for expansion?
3   What is B&Q's growth target?
4   Why is the Chinese market growing so quickly?
5   How does B&Q operate its Chinese stores differently to those in the UK?

3 Are the following statements true or false according to the text?

1   Kingfisher trades under its own name in China.
2   There are over 550 B&Q stores in the world.
3   Kingfisher is Europe's largest electrical retailer.
4   Kingfisher Electricals is based in the UK.
5   The first Asian market B&Q entered was Taiwan.
6   Kingfisher now has 58 stores in the Asia-Pacific region.
7   DIY is traditionally popular in China.
8   The government is investing heavily in housing in Shanghai.
9   B&Q has the same global product lines everywhere in the world.
10 Apartments are very expensive in Shanghai.

4 What do the following words refer to in the text?

1   *its* (line 5)   _____Kingfisher's_____
2   *where* (line 11)   _____
3   *the region* (line 28)   _____
4   *these* (line 29)   _____
5   *it* (line 30)   _____
6   *This growth* (line 33)   _____
7   *such heavy purchases* (line 50)   _____
8   *those in the UK* (line 54)   _____

Vocabulary **5** Match the words from the text with their definitions.

1   enthusiasm   a) expense which is greater than usual
2   slum   b) strong interest in something
3   suburb   c) way of doing something
4   escalator   d) area of housing on the edge of a city
5   format   e) area of very poor housing
6   premium   f) moving walkway or stairs

6 Match the words as they appear in the text.

1   expansion   a) feature
2   market   b) strategy
3   future   c) lines
4   retail   d) standards
5   local   e) giant
6   key   f) growth
7   product   g) needs
8   living   h) position

Vocabulary practice

Trade fairs ❶ Use the clues below to find the eleven trade fair words in the puzzle.

E	X	H	I	B	I	T	I	O	N
B	D	O	T	I	W	E	T	M	E
R	G	I	F	T	S	S	I	A	X
O	E	R	S	E	R	A	C	I	H
C	S	A	M	P	L	E	K	L	I
H	T	H	H	T	L	R	E	O	B
U	A	F	A	A	R	A	T	R	I
R	N	B	R	L	E	T	Y	D	T
E	D	O	T	D	L	Y	O	E	O
M	A	I	L	S	H	O	T	R	R

1 event where things are shown to the public
2 thin glossy booklet giving product information
3 promotional material to show a product attractively
4 things which are given free to customers to promote a product
5 temporary display area that a company constructs at an exhibition
6 service allowing customers to purchase products by post
7 promotional strategy of posting letters to a large number of potential customers
8 you need one to attend an exhibition
9 small example of a product to show what it is like
10 person who displays something at an exhibition
11 large building where trade fairs are held

Commerce ❷ Match the words then use them to complete the sentences below.

long-term ⎯⎯⎯⎯⎯⎯ interests
independent ⎯⎯⎯⎯⎯⎯ commitment
trade retailers
commercial negotiations
entry strategy
intense literature

1 Doing business overseas is a _long-term commitent_ not a way of making quick profits.
2 Do you have any _____ on the product I could take away and read?
3 After several weeks of _____, we finally reached an agreement on price.
4 We don't have our own shops. We sell directly to local _____.
5 Our _____ for getting into the US was to find a joint venture partner.
6 It's a prestigious event and very much in our _____ to exhibit at it.

Writing practice: Using standard letter phrases

Formal letter You work for Meridian Promotions, an exhibition organiser. You have been asked to reply to the enquiry below. Use the following phrases and handwritten notes to write a formal letter of about 200 words.

> please do not hesitate to   we look forward to hearing from you
> we are pleased to confirm that   please find enclosed
> should you have any questions   with reference to

Defrag Software
Mozartplein 44
1042 Amsterdam
The Netherlands

The Bookings Officer
Meridian Promotions
24 Spring Gardens
London W2

Thank him for the enquiry
Dates for 2003: 24–26 October
Enclose booking form and floor plan with available places

12 July 2001

Re: Futuresoft International 2003

Dear Sir / Madam

I am writing to enquire about next year's Futuresoft exhibition. We are a new but fast-growing software developer based in Amsterdam who would be very interested in displaying at the Futuresoft International Exhibition 2003.

We would be very grateful if you could confirm the dates for next year's exhibition and whether there is still exhibition space available. If this is the case, could you please send details of available spots, their prices and a booking form?

As we have not previously exhibited at Futuresoft, we would also be very grateful for any other information about exhibiting, in particular guidelines on display stands and the availability of power etc.

I look forward to hearing from you soon.

Best regards

Application must be in by 1 September and full payment by 1 October
Enclose display stand guidelines
Ask him to submit product information and details of their display stand

Arnold van Rijn
Managing Director
Defrag Software

Technology

Referring to the future

Present tenses can be used to refer to the future in the following ways.

- to describe events that have been arranged (present continuous)
  They're bringing out a new version of the software in March.

- to refer to fixed timetables or schedules (present simple)
  The train doesn't leave until 11.30.

Note! *Will* is not used to describe future arrangements.

We will meet our agents next week.
We're meeting our agents next week.

Going to and *will* can be used to express intentions in the following ways.

- to express existing intentions (*going to* + infinitive)
  We're going to invest $20m in our website next year.

- to express spontaneous intentions (*will* + infinitive)
  A: *Could you send me the report?*
  B: *OK. I'll email you a copy of it.*

Going to, *will* and other modal verbs can be used to make predictions.

- to make predictions based on present evidence (*going to* + infinitive)
  The website's not going to make a profit in the next eighteen months.

- to express future certainty (*will, must*)
  The new system will make a big difference to our resource management.

- to express future probability (*should, would*)
  The increase in teleworking should reduce congestion on the roads.

- to express future possibility (*might, may, could*)
  Worries about security might slow down the growth of e-commerce.

Future perfect and continuous

The future perfect and continuous have the following forms.

will / going to + *have* + past participle
We'll have installed the new system by the time the website goes live.
We're going to have reached 50,000 subscribers by June.

will / going to + *be* + present participle
We'll be doing a lot more training in the near future.
We're going to be investing £800,000 in the new website next quarter.

The future perfect and continuous are used in the following ways.

- to describe actions completed by a certain time in the future
  Our costs will have gone over budget by the end of the month.

- to describe actions in progress at a certain time in the future
  The website won't be ready next week as we'll still be checking it for bugs.

Grammar practice

Futures **1** Complete the sentences with the most appropriate future forms.

1 We _____ our order systems in three months' time.
   a) update   b) will update   c) 're updating
2 I'm absolutely sure that the new design _____ improve sales.
   a) could   b) will   c) should
3 You can't open the attachment? Don't worry. I _____ it again.
   a) send   b) 'll send   c) 'm going to send
4 The flight _____ at ten o'clock in the morning.
   a) leaves   b) will leave   c) is leaving
5 We've decided that we _____ the hardware this year as we can't afford it.
   a) may not upgrade   b) don't upgrade   c) 're not going to upgrade
6 I'm still worried that customers _____ want to give credit card details online.
   a) mightn't   b) mustn't   c) shouldn't

2 Complete the dialogue with the correct future forms.

Pippa   Hey, Richard. (¹you / go) ___Are you going___ to the CeBit conference this year?
Richard We (²all / go) _____, aren't we?
Pippa   No, we're not. They (³cut) _____ the travel budget for the rest of
         the year so only senior sales reps and product development people are allowed
         to go this time.
Richard That (⁴not / be) _____ very popular in the department. A lot of
         people (⁵be) _____ disappointed about not going.
Pippa   You can say that again! I only found out about it this morning from Karen. She
         asked me into her office and told me I can't go.
Richard Is that a final decision?
Pippa   Well, she said there's a chance that she (⁶not / be able to) _____
         go due to other commitments, in which case she (⁷send) _____
         me in her place.
Richard Well, that's better than no chance at all, isn't it?
Pippa   Yeah, but if I (⁸go) _____ in her place, then I (⁹have to)
         _____ do her presentations, too.
Richard Oh right. I see what you mean. That (¹⁰not / be) _____ much fun
         for you! (¹¹she / not / do) _____ our major product presentation
         session?
Pippa   She is! I'm not even sure I want to go any more.

Future perfect **3** Complete the sentences with the future perfect or future continuous form of the verb
and continuous   in brackets.

1 We (already / work) _'ll already be working_ hard on the next version of the program
  when we launch version 2 in March.
2 We (reach) _____ our target of 30,000 registered users of the website
  by the end of the year.
3 They (not / make) _____ any profit on the new phones next year.
4 (you / finish) _____ installing the new software by next week?
5 A lot of telecoms companies (announce) _____ job cuts in order to
  reduce costs over the coming months.
6 By the time the infrastructure upgrade is complete, they (spend) _____
  over $800m.

Reading practice

1 Read the text and answer the questions on the opposite page.

3G - paying the price

As the financial situation worsens for Europe's telecoms, shareholders question whether next-generation mobile phone services can ever produce a return on the massive investment in securing the operating licences.

The struggling European telecoms sector suffered another setback this week as Xfera, the Spanish 3G operator, announced 70 per cent job losses, from 600 employees down to 160. The news follows similar announcements as Europe's major telecoms groups struggle to deal with spiralling debt, plummeting share prices and the delay of 3G - the next generation of mobile phone technology.

3G technology, it is hoped, will generate the next great wave of growth in the mobile phone industry. It will allow mobile phones to receive internet, video and emails faster than by fixed line and modem. With voice traffic set to fall, mobile data services are seen as the future. Major telecoms players hope the new technology will repeat the growth that made mobile phones a fashion icon and the economic success of the 1990s.

However, in order to run 3G networks, these companies needed government licences. Aware of the importance of these licences, governments held auctions and sold them to the highest bidders. The first of these auctions, in the UK, cost the six licenceholders a total of £20bn ($14bn). As this process was repeated across France, Germany and Spain, international telecoms groups were forced to buy several licences in order to operate across Europe. The UK telecoms group BT, for example, paid a total of $30bn. BT argues that it had no choice but to pay what was necessary to secure the licences as without them it would have no future in the industry. '3G is the future of mobile telephony. Without it, you're dead,' says industry analyst Pia Nielson.

Nevertheless, the cost of the licences has driven up debt levels across the European telecoms sector. BT has doubled its debt to £30bn ($21bn) while Deutsche Telekom, its German counterpart, is now $50bn in debt. These huge debts leave licenceholders badly positioned to invest in the infrastructure required to support the new technology. Operators face bills of up to $45bn to improve network quality before they can roll out 3G services on a European basis. Originally scheduled for launch in 2001, widespread 3G access might now be delayed until 2003.

The spiralling debt and delays in bringing the new technology to market have hit shareholder confidence. Within months, BT shares fell from £15 to £5. Similarly, France Telecom and Deutsche Telekom shares have lost 71 and 74 per cent of their value.

It is not only shareholders losing faith in telecoms. Standard & Poor, the credit rating agency, has slashed BT's credit rating from AA plus to A - raising the cost of financing its huge debt. Debt management is now key to the survival of Europe's telecoms, with several companies already disposing of overseas assests to cut debt. Analysts also expect mergers and alliances in the sector and that network sharing will reduce costs.

Another problem facing licenceholders is anticipating customer needs. Will mobile internet services be popular enough for companies to make the licences pay? The mobile phone has established itself as a lifestyle icon just as heavily influenced by fashion as by technological advances. Lifestyle brands such as Nike or Virgin may be better equipped to market 3G services than Europe's global telecoms groups.

However, the major problem will be price. Having paid so much for licences, operators will have to pass this cost on to customers. The telecoms companies were willing to pay the price for 3G. It remains to be seen whether the customer will.

1 What is a 3G mobile phone?

    a) a mobile phone you can use anywhere in the world
    b) a mobile phone that can receive internet and video
    c) a very small and fashionable mobile phone

2 Telecoms companies are so interested in 3G because

    a) the technology will cut their operating costs.
    b) it could give them a competitive advantage.
    c) they think it is the future standard of all mobile phones.

3 Why were the 3G licences so expensive to buy?

    a) Because there is only one licence for each country.
    b) Because governments made companies bid against each other.
    c) Because companies can make huge profits from them.

4 The launch of 3G services will be delayed because

    a) the technology has not been fully developed yet.
    b) not all the government licences have not been sold yet.
    c) networks are not able to operate them yet.

5 What is the biggest problem facing the licenceholders?

    a) how to make the technology work
    b) how to repay the money they owe
    c) how to establish a global presence

6 What will the greatest difficulty be in selling 3G services?

    a) persuading customers to pay a premium for them
    b) giving them a trendy lifestyle image
    c) selling the same services in many different countries

2 **Match the sentence halves.**

1 Companies had to secure 3G licences to	a)	fall dramatically.
2 The delay of 3G has led share prices to	b)	stay in business.
3 Large companies had to buy several licences to	c)	reduce their levels of debt.
4 To buy the licences, the companies had to	d)	pass costs on to the customer.
5 Due to the heavy debt, they are now unable to	e)	maximise revenue from them.
6 Governments auctioned the licences in order to	f)	increase their levels of debt.
7 Companies are selling assets to	g)	implement 3G on schedule.
8 Analysts fear companies will be forced to	h)	operate across Europe.

Vocabulary **3** **The text uses several different words and phrases to refer to the companies and the new technology that the story is about. Read the text again and list them below.**

the companies	the new technology
Europe's telecoms	*3G*
	next-generation mobile phone services

Vocabulary practice

① Complete the word diagram with the following words.

order~~ processing~~   ~~intranet~~   ~~inventories~~   e-commerce   extranet
personalised offerings   telemarketing   supply chain management
teleworking   online billing   vendor   electronic diary   hotdesking

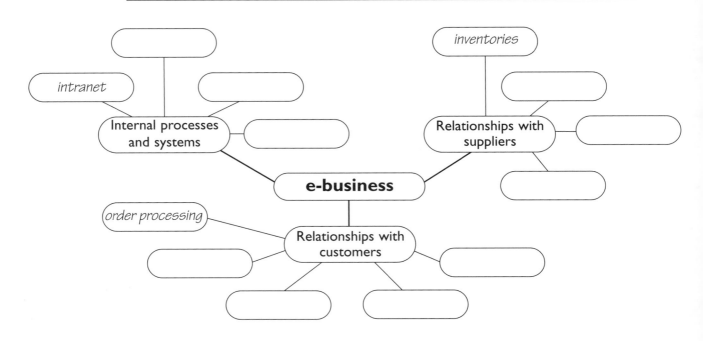

② Match the words then use them to complete the sentences below.

handle   email
personalise   transactions
simplify   processes
anticipate   the system
download   offerings
log onto   wants

1 The new accounting software means we can _handle transactions_ a lot more quickly and get very up-to-date cash flow figures.
2 Our customer profiles allow us to _____ and tailor our services to the cutomers' exact requirements.
3 Each employee has to use a code and password when they _____ in order to protect the security of the central database.
4 The website checks other customers that have bought the same product and what else they've bought. This allows us to _____ and target offerings.
5 Connecting the website to stock data helps us _____ and get goods to customers more quickly. The system for checking stock used to be very complex.
6 We have to put all attachments through a virus detection program whenever we _____ from the internet.

Odd one out ❸ Which word is the odd one out?

1	process	system	plan	routine
2	staff	duties	workers	labour
3	structure	hierarchy	organisation	configuration
4	schedule	inventory	stock	goods
5	key	secure	vital	critical
6	optimise	generate	create	produce

Writing practice: Conciseness

Short report ❶ Match the words in bold with the following features of writing. Which of the features are positive and which should be avoided?

wordiness   reference words   repetition   redundancy

1 Shares in dot.com companies rose quite sharply at the start **of 2000** but then lost a lot of value towards the end **of 2000**.

2 **The new software** allows us to process orders far more quickly. **It** also reduces processing costs by up to 40 per cent.

3 The number of subscribers started at 13,206 in 2001 and only went up **by a very small amount indeed** in the first quarter to 13,895.

4 By giving suppliers access to our extranet, **which we have done**, we have managed to greatly improve the efficiency of our tender system and sourcing processes.

❷ Look at the following report. Although it is factually and grammatically accurate, it is unnecessarily long. Rewrite the report in 120–140 words without changing any facts.

- use reference words
- cut any repetition, redundancy and wordiness

The graph, which is above, shows the total UK sales per day of the week for Millennium Textiles' two best selling product lines – Ladies Office Wear and Ladies Casual Wear. The graph shows that very nearly £90,000 worth of Ladies Office Wear was sold on Mondays during the year 2001. This figure of £90,000 rose quite sharply to a total of £130,000 for Tuesdays. Wednesday and Thursday were very similar indeed with total sales of £140,000 and £135,000. The graph then shows a sharp rise in sales of Ladies Office Wear on Saturday and Sunday. The best day of the week was Saturday with total UK sales of £220,000. Total UK sales on Sundays were very nearly just as high, with a total of £190,000, which is very surprising. Sales of Ladies Casual Wear were quite a bit lower than sales of Ladies Office Wear between Monday and Friday. Only a total of £50,000 worth of Ladies Casual Wear was sold on Mondays in the year 2001. That's £40,000 less than Office Wear on Mondays. The graph shows £60,000 for Tuesdays, £65,000 for Wednesdays, £72,000 for Thursdays and £68,000 for Fridays. Once again there was a big jump at weekends. The company sold a total of £280,000 worth of Ladies Casual Wear on Saturdays in 2001 and almost as much on Sundays – £275,000 worth of items.

Review unit 1 (1–4)

Grammar

1 Complete the dialogue with the correct present, present perfect or past forms.

Geoff OK, let's begin the meeting with a look at some sales figures. Ashok, (¹*you / want*) _____ to start with a look at the Middle East?

Ashok Sure, well, on the whole we (²*do*) _____ quite well. Despite the political events that (³*happen*) _____ recently in the region, sales (⁴*hold*) _____ firm. As you can see from the figures, which I (⁵*copy*) _____ for you here, most of the markets are on target except Jordan.

Ruth What (⁶*happen*) _____ in Jordan?

Ashok Our main distributor, a local company called Jordan Independent Trading, (⁷*go*) _____ out of business in September. As they (⁸*be*) _____ our only sales channel in Jordan, everything (⁹*grind*) _____ to a halt since then, I'm afraid.

Geoff But we (¹⁰*look*) _____ for a new distribution partner since then and it looks like we (¹¹*might / find*) _____ one already.

Ashok That's right. You (¹²*have*) _____ to trade through a local company in Jordan, so without a distribution partner we can't sell at all. We (¹³*currently / negotiate*) _____ with Independent Trading's main rival, who (¹⁴*be*) _____ now one of the biggest importers in the country.

Ruth (¹⁵*you / know*) _____ Jordan Independent Trading was going out of business?

Ashok We (¹⁶*know*) _____ there were problems, of course. But it all (¹⁷*happen*) _____ a lot quicker than we expected.

Ruth What about our stock in Independent's warehouse?

Ashok Jordan isn't really a big market for us so the distributor usually (¹⁸*not / keep*) _____ high stock levels. As for the stock they (¹⁹*have*) _____, we really (²⁰*not / know*) _____ what's going to happen to it.

Geoff I (²¹*not / think*) _____ that's a big issue really. The important thing is we (²²*already / take*) _____ steps to open up a fresh sales channel and, as Ashok (²³*say*) _____ at the start, the rest of the region (²⁴*have*) _____ an excellent last twelve months.

Ruth I (²⁵*agree*) _____. I was just wondering what the procedure was in such cases, that's all.

Geoff That's OK. So, thank you, Ashok. Shall we move on now to Martina and Latin America? Martina ....

2 Complete the sentences with an appropriate relative pronoun.

1 It must be very difficult for a lot of older managers _____ just aren't very computer literate.

2 There's no point in updating a system _____ is working perfectly well if you're not having any problems with it.

3 The latest version of the program, _____ was released in July, still seems to be full of bugs.

4 We'll need to hire someone _____ experience includes working with Powerpoint.

5 Make sure we buy software _____ is compatible with our existing software and will run smoothly on the network.

6 The program _____ I really want is just too expensive, unfortunately.

7 It was installed by the young engineer _____ was here yesterday.

8 I think it's the memory _____ is the problem. Your computer just doesn't have enough of it to run the program. You'll need to upgrade it.

9 I can't really help you, I'm afraid. You'll have to find someone _____ knowledge of Excel is better than mine.

10 Press the ESCAPE key, _____ is top left of your keyboard, and you'll return to the previous order screen. That's it.

3 Complete the report with the correct form of adjective or adverb.

Microsoft Corporation 24 Month Share Price (as of 4/1/2002)

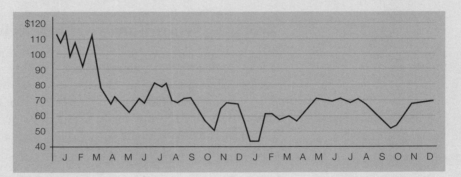

The Microsoft share price began 2000 at just over $110. Over the next three months it fluctuated (¹*dramatic*) _____, falling as low as $90 before returning to its (²*original*) _____ level. However, in March 2000 it (³*sudden*) _____ plummeted, losing over $40 by April. Although the speed of the fall slowed (⁴*slight*) _____, it continued down to $60 by May. A (⁵*brief*) _____ recovery took the price back to $80, where it remained (⁶*stable*) _____ until July. It then started to decline (⁷*steady*) _____ over the next three months, falling as (⁸*low*) _____ as $50 by November. The year 2000 ended more (⁹*encouraging*) _____ for Microsoft with shares back at the $70. However, 2001 started (¹⁰*bad*) _____ with shares dropping to a two-year low of $43 by the end of January. A (¹¹*reasonable*) _____ (¹²*quick*) _____ recovery took shares back above $60 in February and further (¹³*steady*) _____ progress saw them back above $70 by May. Unfortunately, prices fell (¹⁴*sharp*) _____ again, back down to almost $50 by October. The shares recovered (¹⁵*good*) _____ over the last two months to finish at the $70 mark. So, despite a difficult 2001 for Microsoft with the federal court case, shares finished at the same level as they started the year.

4 Complete the sentences with the correct present or future form.

1 They (*reveal*) _____ the name of the new CEO on Tuesday when they (*make*) _____ the official announcement about the merger.

2 They (*cut*) _____ jobs as soon as the merger (*be*) _____ complete.

3 They (*not / be able*) _____ to proceed with the merger until the European Competition Commissioner (*approve*) _____ it.

4 We (*not / release*) _____ any details of the planned merger to the press while negotiations (*take*) _____ place.

5 We (*need*) _____ to conclude the deal before they (*receive*) _____ a better offer from someone else.

6 The unions (*not / make*) _____ a statement until they (*read*) _____ the details of the takeover.

7 They (*find*) _____ it hard to fight a hostile takeover bid while their share price (*fall*) _____ the way it is.

8 When the deal (*go*) _____ through, we (*be*) _____ the third largest bank in the country.

9 We (*not / know*) _____ if the deal is successful until they (*have*) _____ two or three years' trading as a fully-merged company.

10 We really (*need*) _____ to reduce the company's unacceptable level of debt before we (*look*) _____ for a buyer.

5 Complete the report extract with *a, an, the* or no article (Ø).

Working from home – a feasibility study

It is clear that ¹_____ nature of our business means that ²_____ good number of staff should be able to work from home. As long as ³_____ employee has ⁴_____ access to our web-based intranet, they will be able to work easily with ⁵_____ company database. It is also possible to re-route ⁶_____ telephone calls so callers are automatically redirected to staff homes.

Almost forty per cent of ⁷_____ staff have expressed ⁸_____ interest in working from home. Of these, fifteen per cent would like to work from their homes on ⁹_____ full-time basis, while ¹⁰_____ other twenty-five per cent would like ¹¹_____ flexibility to work from home two or three days each week, as and when it is convenient.

Each employee who enquired about working from home was asked to complete ¹²_____ job profile and technical audit in order to assess the level of ¹³_____ IT support they would require. If ¹⁴_____ company is genuinely serious about encouraging ¹⁵_____ employees to work from home, then it will definitely need to consider how it intends to provide 24-hour IT support to these employees in their homes.

---

6 Complete the dialogue with appropriate future forms.

Luisa Hi Pia. How are you?

Pia Oh, OK. It's all a bit hectic at the moment. You know with the sales conference and everything.

Luisa It's that time of year again, isn't it? (¹you /go) _____ to the conference?

Pia Yes, everyone in Marketing is. And this year (²be) _____ the biggest conference yet.

Luisa Where (³it /hold) _____ this year?

Pia It's Helsinki, two weeks on Monday.

Luisa So soon? (⁴you /fly) _____ out on the Monday morning or the day before?

Pia The Monday morning flight (⁵leave) _____ at something like six o'clock in the morning. I (⁶not /get) _____ up at 3.30 am just to catch a plane, so I (⁷fly) _____ out on Sunday evening.

Luisa I don't blame you. It is a bit early, isn't it? And (⁸you /do) _____ any presentations at the conference?

Pia I (⁹do) _____ two product presentations on the Tuesday morning. But I (¹⁰also /help) _____ Marco with his sessions on Wednesday.

Luisa How many people (¹¹be) _____ at your presentations?

Pia I'm not sure really. All the national managers (¹²be) _____ there. And there (¹³be) _____ the marketing people too, of course. So, I guess something like 200 people.

Luisa Rather you than me. I think I (¹⁴enjoy) _____ a nice quiet week at the office without any managers around!

Pia Sounds lovely. I know one thing for sure – it (¹⁵not /be) _____ quiet in Helsinki.

7 Complete the sentences with the future continuous or future perfect form of the verbs in brackets.

1 I'm on the train right now just outside Lyon. So I (arrive) _____ in about twenty minutes.

2 Two weeks skiing in the USA! You lucky thing. I (think) _____ of you while I'm sitting at my desk all next week.

3 We (not /finish) _____ the report by next Monday.

4 (you /visit) _____ suppliers while you're in India?

5 If we're not careful, our rivals (launch) _____ their own products before ours hits the market.

6 The schedule's very tight, so we (not /do) _____ any sightseeing while we're in Barcelona.

7 You'd better call them first thing Monday because they (not /hear) _____ the news by then.

8 High development costs mean they (not /make) _____ any profit on their new product in the first two years.

9 If we keep losing money at this rate, we (lose) _____ over half a billion dollars by the end of the year.

10 Now the companies have merged, they (look) _____ at ways of reducing their costs.

Vocabulary

Complete each sentence with the correct option.

1. We need to _____ our objectives before we start planning the campaign.
   a) clarify   b) interpret   c) prescribe
2. After Apple's success with the iMac, PC producers jumped on the _____ .
   a) trend   b) hype   c) bandwagon
3. We have to be clear about customer _____ of what our product stands for.
   a) branding   b) perceptions   c) values
4. Many supermarkets are looking to _____ into new product lines.
   a) deregulate   b) destabilise   c) diversify
5. We've got a very _____ management structure that won't be easy to change.
   a) rigid   b) nimble   c) rapid
6. What we're looking for is loyalty and _____ from our shareholders.
   a) enterprise   b) commitment   c) congestion
7. We want to _____ new reporting procedures to improve communication.
   a) initiate   b) motivate   c) brief
8. Employees working from home have secure access to the company _____ .
   a) internet   b) extranet   c) intranet
9. We reviewed our _____ processes and cut production times by 12 per cent.
   a) management   b) sales   c) operating
10. We're _____ the company on the FTSE to raise capital for expansion.
    a) sharing   b) selling   c) floating
11. They need to _____ two very different cultures to make the merger work.
    a) integrate   b) implement   c) join
12. The companies announced _____ merger worth $20bn.
    a) a non-cash   b) an all-share   c) a swap
13. We'll need to set up the exhibition _____ the day before the fair opens.
    a) showcase   b) store   c) stand
14. We bought an address list and did a _____ of 2,500 addresses.
    a) posting   b) mailshot   c) send-off
15. The company faced a hostile takeover when its shares _____ on the NYSE.
    a) dipped   b) plummeted   c) peaked
16. Be careful of viruses when you _____ email from people you don't recognise.
    a) download   b) connect   c) log onto
17. It was hard to get used to such a _____ different culture when I was in Japan.
    a) slightly   b) basically   c) radically
18. The meeting lasted all night due to the _____ of the negotiations.
    a) disparity   b) complexity   c) flexibility
19. Many dotcoms went bankrupt when the internet bubble finally _____ .
    a) deflated   b) burst   c) broke
20. We need to find ways of _____ our customers' wants more effectively.
    a) anticipating   b) guessing   c) considering
21. They're cutting management jobs in order to _____ their company structure.
    a) shrink   b) streamline   c) economise
22. The international trade fair is a _____ event for companies to exhibit at.
    a) fundamental   b) diverse   c) prestigious
23. We don't have a sales force of our own. We use _____ agents.
    a) third-party   b) independent   c) free
24. The software wasn't _____ with our system so we had to replace it.
    a) interactive   b) interconnected   c) compatible
25. Demand has been very _____ so we're cutting prices to stimulate sales.
    a) inflated   b) static   c) even
26. Our ability to respond to changes has been _____ by a lack of information.
    a) refined   b) depressed   c) hampered

27 Due to large losses, shareholders won't receive a _____ this year.
    a) dividend   b) bonus   c) revenue

28 In China it's very _____ to arrive late for a meeting.
    a) hospitable   b) discourteous   c) harmonious
29 Smart companies are pushing social issues up the _____ .
    a) schedule   b) agenda   c) itinerary
30 We publish _____ on the net and invite suppliers to send quotes.
    a) specifications   b) findings   c) expectations
31 Despite early losses, they managed to _____ by the end of the year.
    a) stabilise   b) level out   c) break even
32 We ordered 500 12-page glossy _____ to hand out at the trade fair.
    a) leaflets   b) brochures   c) samples
33 We don't own the Paris office. We _____ it from a larger company.
    a) hire   b) borrow   c) lease
34 There are several important issues _____ from the findings of this report.
    a) arising   b) coming   c) attributing
35 They had to sell off some _____ in order to reduce their level of debt.
    a) headquarters   b) assets   c) capital
36 Our customers buy our goods from independent high street _____ .
    a) wholesalers   b) distributors   c) retailers
37 By _____, we've been able to reduce our office space by 20 per cent.
    a) swapping desks   b) desk exchange   c) hotdesking
38 The joint venture has been a successful _____ for both parties.
    a) collaboration   b) teamwork   c) interaction
39 The price of the shares was _____ by the lack of their availability.
    a) inflated   b) generated   c) enhanced
40 The investment in new point-of-sale _____ boosted sales by 12 per cent.
    a) showcases   b) stands   c) displays
41 In future companies will have to face up to their social _____ more.
    a) expectations   b) agendas   c) obligations
42 Do you know how much of the budget has been _____ to recruitment?
    a) ensured   b) allocated   c) prescribed
43 Flexible working lets us _____ labour to meet peaks and troughs in demand.
    a) process   b) schedule   c) transform
44 The major _____ reduced the company's market capitalisation by 70 per cent.
    a) selling   b) sale   c) sell-off
45 Many companies now no longer allow employees to accept _____ .
    a) gadgets   b) gimmicks   c) gifts
46 They're trying to reduce the layers of _____ and do away with status symbols.
    a) structure   b) hierarchy   c) organisation
47 The email system should help us improve _____ within the company.
    a) communication   b) information   c) interconnectivity
48 We sold our _____ in RoyalMed to focus on our core activities.
    a) partition   b) presence   c) equity stake
49 The new warehouse system allows us to manage our _____ a lot better.
    a) inventory   b) assets   c) holdings
50 A recent wave of _____ has left only five big players in the market.
    a) joint ventures   b) efficiencies   c) consolidation

Human resources

Passive

Form   The passive has the following forms.

subject + correct tense of the verb *be* + past participle
*Most vacancies **are filled** by internal applicants.*
*The position **was advertised** on the Internet.*
*Staff motivation **has been affected** by the job cuts.*
*The vacancy **won't be filled** until next month.*
*Where **is** the interview **being held**?*

Use   The passive is used in the following ways.

- when the agent is unimportant or unknown
  *Staff wages **have been increased** by 4 per cent.*

- to describe systems and processes
  *All senior appointments **are managed** by an executive search agency.*

- to create an impersonal or formal style
  *A shortlist of four candidates **has been compiled**. I enclose their CVs.*

Reference words

The following can refer to other parts of a text.

- *one / ones*
  *We're advertising several grades of vacancies at the moment. However, you'll only see the lower level **ones** advertised internally.*

- *former / latter*
  *The position was advertised in a national newspaper and on the internet. The **former** resulted in very few applications, whereas the **latter** produced a substantial number of completely unsuitable responses.*

- *such*
  *There has been a steady increase in absenteeism levels recently. It is clear that **such** a trend cannot be tolerated any further.*

- determiners (*this, that, these, those*)
  *We received a shortlist of three candidates. Each of **these** was interviewed by both the recruitment agency and ourselves.*
  *The management recently cut bonuses. **This** has caused a certain amount of ill-feeling in the Sales Department.*

Note!   *This* followed by a noun refers back to the previous noun, whereas *this* without a following noun refers back to the previous idea.

*The company has decided to reward employees with an **extra six per cent pay increase**. **This bonus** should have a positive effect on employee morale. **The jobs will be advertised on the web page**. It is hoped that **this** will increase the number of applicants.*

The ones has the same meaning as *those* but is less formal.

*Where are the reports? You know, **the ones** we were looking at earlier.*

Grammar practice

Passive ❶ Rewrite the sentences using the passive. Do not change the tenses.

1 We advertised the jobs in the *Guardian* last month.
   The jobs were advertised in the Guardian last month.

2 Can you tell me how many vacancies you're going to advertise?
   _____

3 I'm sorry but we've just filled that particular vacancy.
   _____

4 We won't recruit a new manager until next year.
   _____

5 They normally hold appraisal interviews in January.
   _____

6 We haven't processed all the applications yet.
   _____

7 When did they interview you?
   _____

8 Have you seen how many jobs they're advertising on their website?
   _____

❷ Complete the report extract with the correct active or passive forms.

It (¹*find*) *has been found* that motivation within the Customer Service Department (²*seriously / affect*) _____ by the recent restructuring and the consequent redundancies. Although only two people (³*make*) _____ redundant from the department, the remaining team members (⁴*feel*) _____ that their jobs (⁵*threaten*) _____ by the changes. Another major concern that (⁶*voice*) _____ by employees is that of staff (⁷*place*) _____ under increased pressure as workloads (⁸*increase*) _____ to cover the duties of those who (⁹*leave*) _____ the department. Furthermore, there is also a feeling that the changes (¹⁰*not / make*) _____ particularly logically and they (¹¹*handle*) _____ insensitively by management. It is therefore clear that motivation and goodwill (¹²*not /restore*) _____ easily or quickly.

Reference words ❸ Use the following reference words to complete the note below.

| ~~those~~ the latter these ones those the former such this ones |

Geoff
I looked through all ¹ *those* applications you gave me. It took forever! I soon started putting them into groups – ² _____ worth reading carefully and the rest, which were completely unsuitable. Unfortunately, ³ _____ far outnumbered ⁴ _____ . I know ⁵ _____ is usually the case with recruitment, but is it me or is the standard of applications getting worse nowadays? I couldn't even read half of the handwritten ⁶ _____ . How can ⁷ _____ applicants ever hope to get an interview? Thankfully, once I started looking through the better ⁸ _____ , it was more encouraging. I've noted about six applicants I'd like to invite for interview. From ⁹ _____ I'd hope to make a shortlist of about three for a second interview with Elizabeth.

Reading practice

1 Read the text and match the paragraphs (1–7) with the headings on the opposite page.

PERSONNEL

'Site currently down – more information soon'

The simple six-word message that signalled the end of Stepstone, the high-profile UK online recruitment company.

1 Stepstone, the European online recruiter, announced this week that it was to shut down all UK operations, raising doubts about the future of the online recruitment sector. The Norwegian-owned company is to cut 525 jobs from its 876 strong work-force and concentrate on its markets in Denmark, Germany and Belgium.

2 One of the most widely-known brands in the industry, Stepstone was famous for its £7m sponsorship of televised sport on Channel 4 in the UK. Despite such healthy brand recognition and its website carrying 14,000 vacancies, mounting losses have forced the company into liquidation.

3 Stepstone announced third quarter losses of £10m, down from £25m the previous quarter. The losses are large for a company rapidly running out of cash. Like many other dotcoms, Stepstone expanded aggressively and burnt through shareholder capital far more quickly than its business model was able to generate profits. In the six months to September, cash reserves fell from £30m to just £14m. The company's shares have fallen just as dramatically, from 62 Norwegian Kroner in March to just 0.3 Kroner at the time of the latest announcement.

4 With the collapse of Stepstone's market value, investors are questioning whether there is any money at all to be made from dotcom recruitment. However, analyst Claudia Silvino is convinced that online job hunting is here to stay: 'Online recruitment is the ideal application of internet technology. Jobhunters can search through thousands of vacancies quickly and efficiently and they can register CVs for the attention of thousands of companies at a fraction of the cost of posting them individually. There are over one million vacancies on the internet in the UK at the moment. The problem is that there are also well over a thousand recruitment websites. The industry will survive but Stepstone won't be the last to go under.'

5 Despite the failure of Stepstone, the size of the UK online recruitment market looks set to increase. Monster, the UK's largest online recruiter, now holds over 300,000 CVs on its database. More and more companies now see the internet as vital to their recruitment strategy. 'Within five years, all jobs will be advertised only on the internet,' argues Silvino. Ryanair, the UK low-cost airline, already refuses to handle anything but online applications. 'Don't ring, don't fax, don't post; this is the only way your application will be processed,' says its website.

6 However, Mark Fischer, a headhunter for London-based Elite, doesn't see online recruitment as suitable for every vacancy. 'You might not want your competitors to know that you're looking to replace a key executive. Sensitive hirings can only be done by a headhunter so the internet has no direct use for us.' There is also the issue of security. Ryanair's 'online only' policy hit the news when it was discovered that applicants had to submit personal information and credit card numbers through a non-secure website. 'A lot of people still just don't trust the internet,' says Fischer.

7 Whether the growth in online recruitment will be enough to tempt investors back to companies like Stepstone remains to be seen. New Chief Executive Colin Tenwick is hoping to raise fresh finance. Shareholders, meanwhile, are very aware that business is currently down and are waiting for more information soon.

a) Stepstone's financial position
b) the UK online recruitment market
c) a profile of Stepstone
d) the future of Stepstone
e) introduction   *paragraph 1*
f) the future of online recruitment in the UK
g) reasons for not recruiting online

2 **Read the text again and answer the questions.**

1 How did Stepstone get into financial difficulty?
2 What effect has it had on the UK online recruitment market?
3 What is the future for UK online recruitment market?
4 What are the advantages and disadvantages of online recruitment?
5 What is Stepstone's future strategy?

3 **Read the text again and complete the sentences below with the following.**

~~Ryanair~~   Stepstone   Monster   Elite   Channel 4

1 You can only apply for jobs at _____*Ryanair*_____ through their website.
2 _____ is the UK's largest online recruitment company.
3 _____ does not use the internet to recruit for client companies.
4 _____ received a lot of money from _____ in sponsorship.
5 _____ has a Norwegian parent company.
6 The headquarters of _____ are in London.
7 _____ is a television company.
8 _____ was in the news because of the lack of security on its website.

4 **Read the text again and complete the information about Stepstone.**

	six months ago	now
employees	876	
share price		
markets		
cash reserves		

5 **Match the words from the text with their definitions.**

1 doubt   a) money a company has for investment
2 sponsorship   b) feeling of uncertainty
3 recognition   c) small part of something
4 liquidation   d) money a company keeps back for future use
5 capital   e) financial support for a TV / radio station in return for advertising
6 reserves   f) awareness
7 fraction   g) bankruptcy

Vocabulary practice

Odd one out **1** Which word does not go with the word in capital letters?

1 JOB
   rotation   satisfaction   behaviour   enrichment
2 STAFF
   motivation   criteria   car park   feedback
3 TEAM
   appointee   spirit   building   leader
4 EXECUTIVE
   search   forces   position   salary
5 ONLINE
   newsgroup   advertising   recruitment   candidate

Headhunting **2** Put the following stages of the headhunting process in the correct order.

❑ a) The headhunter assists with the final contract negotiations.
❑ b) The headhunter researches potential companies to identify candidates.
❑ c) The client pays the headhunter the final balance of his / her fee.
❑ d) The headhunter interviews potential candidates and draws up a shortlist.
❑ e) The client instructs the headhunter to fill a vacancy and pays a retainer.
❑ f) The headhunter presents findings to the client.
❑ g) The client interviews the most promising candidates from the shortlist.
❑ h) The headhunter targets individuals within these companies.
❑ i) The client pays the second instalment of the headhunter's fee.
❑ j) The chosen candidate signs a contract of employment.

Prefixes **3** Put each adjective in the correct group according to the prefix that forms its opposite.
Then use the positive or negative forms to complete the sentences below.

| competent   ethical   formal   satisfactory   discreet |
| appropriate   co-operative   flexible   enthusiastic |

in-	*un-*
incompetent	

1 He's _incompetent_ ! He just doesn't know how to do the job properly!
2 She's a very _____ member of the team – always willing to help people.
3 Wasim was pretty _____ about his promotion. He didn't look happy at all.
4 This is just an _____ spoken warning. Next time it will go on your record.
5 Your promotion might upset some people so be _____ about it for a while.
6 If the terms of the contract are _____, please sign and return it to us.
7 Li can be a bit _____ at times and needs to try doing things differently.
8 We'll never recruit a top manager, offering such an _____ salary.
9 Exploiting company expenses is at least _____ and possibly a sacking offence.

Writing practice: Formal language

Standard phrases ❶ Match the informal spoken phrases with the formal written phrases.

1	What about ...	a)	It was agreed that ...
2	It looks as if ...	b)	It is suggested that ...
3	If I were you, I'd ...	c)	A further issue is ...
4	We've got problems with ...	d)	We recommend that ...
5	We decided to ...	e)	It would seem that ...
6	Another thing is ...	f)	The following areas of concern have been highlighted.

Formal report ❷ You have been asked to write a report on your company's staffing requirements. Use the information below to write a report of 200-250 words. Consider your reader and purpose and use an appropriate level of formality. Include the following information.

- the number of new people each department needs

- the kind of candidates that are needed

- how these people should be recruited

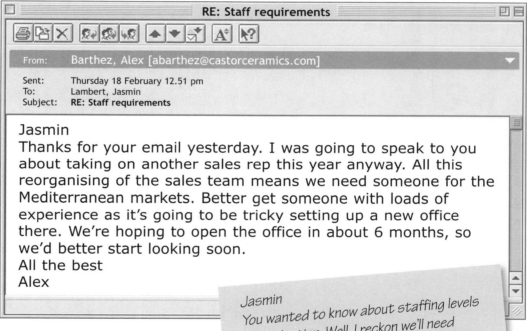

RE: Staff requirements

From: Barthez, Alex [abarthez@castorceramics.com]

Sent: Thursday 18 February 12.51 pm
To: Lambert, Jasmin
Subject: RE: Staff requirements

Jasmin
Thanks for your email yesterday. I was going to speak to you about taking on another sales rep this year anyway. All this reorganising of the sales team means we need someone for the Mediterranean markets. Better get someone with loads of experience as it's going to be tricky setting up a new office there. We're hoping to open the office in about 6 months, so we'd better start looking soon.
All the best
Alex

Jasmin
You wanted to know about staffing levels in production. Well, I reckon we'll need another five people for holiday cover this summer. George is retiring next year so it might be an idea to keep a couple of them on afterwards even.
Javagal

Jasmin
Thanks for the note about secretarial resourcing. If you ask me, I think we'll need to look at a couple of new people. Martha is going on maternity leave soon and we don't know yet whether she's coming back afterwards. And there's always holidays, of course. Could we advertise for two new secretarial staff? If we advertise locally, it'll be cheap and then we can train them up.
Louise

Culture

Gerunds and infinitives

Gerunds (-*ing* forms) are used in the following ways.

- as nouns
  *We've started offering cultural awareness **training** to our staff.*

- after prepositions and certain verbs (see the list on page 66)
  *We don't send staff abroad **without giving** them a culture briefing first.*
  *I really **enjoy learning** about new cultures and different countries.*

Infinitives are used in the following ways.

- after certain verbs (see the list on page 66)
  *We can't **afford not to give** our managers cross-cultural awareness training.*

- after adjectives (often with *too* or *enough*)
  *All our staff are **confident enough to give** feedback to their managers.*

- after nouns
  *We're under a lot of **pressure to cut** costs.*

Note! Some verbs can be followed by either a gerund or an infinitive.

- with no difference (*begin, hate, like, love, prefer, start*)
  *I **hate spending / to spend** so much time away from home.*

- with a time difference (*forget, remember, regret*)
  *Do you **remember meeting** Mr Solanki in Lahore?* (refers to the past)
  ***Remember to pick up** the market report.* (refers to the present / future)

Modal verbs

Modal verbs are used in the following ways.

- to express intentions (*will, might, could* – also *going to*)
  *We**'ll** / **'re going to** / **might make** an announcement soon.*

- to express permission (*may, can, could* – also *allowed to*)
  ***May / Can / Could** I **have** Spanish lessons before I leave for Mexico?*

- to express ability (*can, could* – also *able to*)
  *They **couldn't / were unable to deal** with cultural differences after the merger.*

- to make spontaneous offers (*will, can, shall*)
  *We**'ll adapt** the product if it isn't selling well in Italy.*

- to make suggestions (*should, shall, could*)
  ***Should / Shall** I **phone** them to ask about dietary requirements?*

- to make requests (*can, could, would, may*)
  ***Can / Could / Would** you **send** a copy of our values to all managers, please?*
  ***May** I **use** your phone, please?*

- to express obligation (*must, should* – also *have to*)
  *All foreign companies **must / should / have to have** a local partner.*

- to express different levels of possibility (see page 24)
  *We**'ll** / **might** / **could use** the same catalogue in Japan.*

Grammar practice

Gerunds and infinitives

1 Complete the dialogue with the correct form of the verbs in brackets.

Rod   Hi, Sandra. How are you? How's the new job going?

Sandra   Fine, thanks. The job's going OK.

Rod   I think (¹leave) _____*leaving*_____ like you did caused one or two of us to think about our own positions too, you know. So, anyway, what's it like (²work) _____ for MegaCorp? Do they expect staff (³do) _____ as many hours as everyone says they do?

Sandra   Oh, it's not too bad. You're under a lot of pressure (⁴meet) _____ deadlines. But it used (⁵be) _____ like that anyway, didn't it?

Rod   That's true. Do you remember (⁶work) _____ on that contract for Pakistan? I can't believe the number of extra hours we must have put in.

Sandra   I know. But we managed (⁷get) _____ it done on time. So life's not really that much different at MegaCorp.

Rod   And what about the people? Are they nice (⁸work) _____ with?

Sandra   Yeah. It's always difficult (⁹make) _____ friends at a new company, isn't it? But it's such a relief (¹⁰not / have) _____ to work for Charles Osbourne any more! I hated (¹¹have) _____ to do all those stupid little jobs he gave me. Not to mention always (¹²have) _____ to show him how to use his computer. At least my new boss actually appears (¹³know) _____ how to use his!

Rod   No, you didn't really get on with Charles, did you?

Sandra   I know. I couldn't wait (¹⁴leave) _____, could I? But I just couldn't carry on (¹⁵be) _____ so unhappy at work every day. Anyway, how are you? How are things back at Global?

Modal verbs

2 Rewrite the following sentences using a modal verb.

1 Maybe we'll offer cultural awareness training to sales executives.
   We might offer cultural awareness training to sales executives.

2 Why don't we take our overseas guests to a sporting event?
   _____

3 We'll be obliged to socialise with our hosts during our stay in Japan.
   _____

4 Is it possible to drink alcohol in the hotel?
   _____

5 We didn't manage to set up a meeting with Mr Tse.
   _____

6 Is it all right if I bring a colleague with me to the meeting?
   _____

3 Choose the correct verb form to complete each sentence.

1 You *don't have to / mustn't* drink alcohol in public while you're there.

2 We *wouldn't / couldn't* reach agreement with a suitable local partner.

3 *Will / Shall* I arrange some sandwiches for lunch?

4 There *might / will* be difficulties integrating the two companies. Only time will tell.

5 I'm sorry you didn't get the report. I *'ll / 'm going to* send it to you right away.

6 UK citizens *don't have to / mustn't* get a visa for travelling to the USA.

7 What *might you / are you going to* do with the Nigerian visitors?

8 *May / Would* I use your phone, please?

❶ Read the text and match the paragraphs with the questions on the opposite page.

Clash of the Titans

After Mannesmann loses its fight against Vodafone's hostile takeover, is Germany about to lose more than just ownership of one of its most famous companies? **Jamilla Ahktar** *reports.*

1 After a bitter three-month conflict, Vodafone, the world's largest mobile phone company, looks set to complete its $180bn hostile takeover of Mannesmann, Germany's largest mobile phone operator. The deal is Germany's first ever hostile takeover by a foreign company and has led to warnings that German business culture itself is now under threat from foreign invaders. Mannesmann's Chairman, Klaus Esser, claimed that the company's shareholders had neglected long-term prospects in favour of their own short-term financial reward.

2 Resistance to the deal has been widespread in Germany. Mannesmann workers demonstrated outside the company's Düsseldorf headquarters, fearing that aggressive Anglo-American business culture will lead to extensive job cuts. Klaus Ulrich, spokesman for IG Metall, Germany's largest engineering union, also sees Vodafone as a danger to Mannesmann's consensual business culture: 'What we fear from Vodafone is that our business culture, which takes account of the interests of workers as well as shareholders and has been developed over the years, will be destroyed.' Chancellor Gerhard Schroeder has also said that hostile takeovers damage corporate culture.

3 The system that Schroeder and the unions see under threat is based on a consensus between closely-integrated institutions such as banks, employers, union and government – a system that they see as key to Germany's economic success. Companies have long-term relationships with banks, whose executives sit on the companies' supervisory boards. Companies within the same industry form sector associations, which not only agree industry-wide wage settlements with the unions but also fix vocational training standards to equip workers with industry-specific skills. There is also widespread sharing of research resources. Labour market regulation, enforced by the German government, employers and unions, discourages companies from using job cuts to combat short-term economic downturns. Any major strategic decision must be made in full consultation with powerful workers' councils.

4 In contrast to this system of values is the so-called Anglo-American economic model preferred in the USA and UK. In these countries, market forces regulate relationships between banks and companies, and employers and workers. Finance and labour markets are fluid. Highly developed financial markets make it easy for companies to raise capital and deregulated labour markets allow companies to hire and fire workers according to short-term sales performance. However, there is little incentive for companies to invest in the long-term development of employees' skills. In the USA and UK, employees are also often left to negotiate their own pay levels.

5 Both business cultures have their merits. Although the German system produces stability, it is bureaucratic and suffers from slow decision-making. The German model creates the long-term technical knowledge vital for engineering, whereas the Anglo-American system succeeds in dynamic environments where change is continuous and a fast response essential. The Daimler-Benz takeover of Chrysler illustrates the success of German automobile manufacturing; however, the high-tech, ever-changing world of Formula One motor racing is dominated by UK engineering.

6 Resistance to the Vodafone/Mannesmann deal clearly shows the German desire to defend their business culture. Whether the system will be able to withstand the attack of globalisation and European deregulation, however, remains to be seen. German companies will need to ensure that their share prices perform as well as US rivals in order to protect themselves from foreign raiders and to finance acquisitions of their own. This will make it harder for companies to offer long-term employment. There is also a fundamental shift in the European economies away from heavy mechanical engineering, in which Germany excels, towards dynamic high-tech, knowledge-based industries, such as biotechnology, that require constant innovation.

7 Despite his objections to hostile takeovers, Chancellor Schroeder is under increasing pressure to increase economic flexibility. Recent tax reforms included measures allowing banks to sell their stakes in companies tax-free, encouraging them to break with long-term partner companies and redirect capital towards growth industries of the future. Whether the German banks will choose to do so remains to be seen.

a) What is a 'consensual business culture'? *paragraph 3*
b) Why is Vodafone's takeover of Mannesmann so unusual?
c) Why will it be difficult for Germany to defend its system?
d) What is an 'Anglo-American' business culture?
e) What changes in regulation has the German government made?
f) What are the advantages of each type of culture?
g) Why is German industry so unhappy about the takeover?

2 Read the description of German business culture again and identify the relationships between the following institutions in German business.

1	supervisory boards	banks	*Bank executives sit on supervisory boards.*
2	employers	workers' councils	_____
3	sector associations	unions	_____
4	government	unions	_____

3 The text describes German and 'Anglo-American' business culture. Read the following statements and decide who might say them and which culture they refer to.

1 'We've dealt with them for many years now. We're happy to provide capital when they need it. It's a close working relationship and they keep us informed at all times.'

2 'I have to negotiate my own pay rises by myself. The union doesn't have enough power to negotiate on behalf of all of us so there's not a lot you can do if you're badly paid.'

3 'Although we're competitors, it clearly makes sense for us to share the cost of basic research. If it raises the standards of all our products, then it's in all our interests.'

4 'We strongly believe in training and the standardisation of skills. If all workers have good skills, then it makes recruitment easier for all of us in the industry.'

5 'We have absolutely no role in strategic decision-making. The management just make a decision and then tell us what's going to happen. It's even possible to see your own job advertised in the newspaper before you're told what's happening.'

6 'If orders are down, then we have to save money and make some people redundant. If we couldn't, then we'd go out of business. Flexibility's the key to survival.'

7 'We don't have a large influence on how the company makes its decisions but we do have a couple of senior executives on the supervisory board. They're there to keep us informed about what the company's doing and to make sure they act responsibly.'

8 'Advertising is a very dynamic industry, so we do need to keep our options open and be able to recruit when business is good and cut costs when it isn't.'

9 'Nobody believes in a job for life any more. And when a company can just make you redundant tomorrow, why should you stay loyal to them all your career?'

Vocabulary **4** The text uses a lot of war metaphors. Find other words in the text with a similar meaning as the following.

1	clash	*conflict*
2	aggressive	_____
3	danger	_____
4	destroy	_____
5	fight	_____
6	protect	_____
7	resist	_____
8	invaders	_____

Vocabulary practice

Culture **1** Complete the word diagram with the following words.

~~mission statement~~   cultural values   positioning   policies
products   dress code   basic values   status symbols   mindset
organisational hierarchy   uniform   value systems

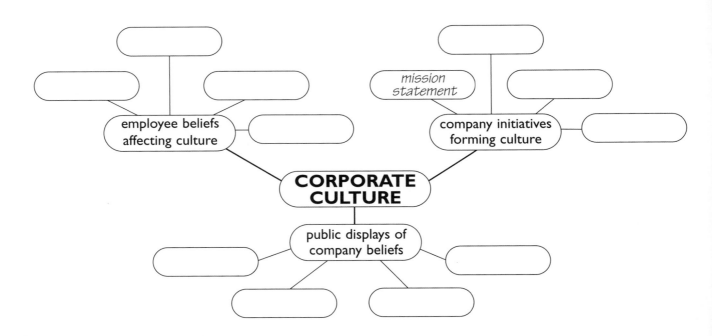

2 Complete the table then use the words to complete the sentences below.

adjective	noun
diverse	_diversity_
_____	vitality
_____	optimism
humble	_____
valid	_____
cost-conscious	_____

1 The ____diversity____ of our workforce means we do a lot of cultural awareness work.
2 I admire your _____ but I can't see us achieving those sales figures.
3 Sales are up but so is expenditure. We need to be more _____ in future.
4 She's so full of energy and her _____ gets the whole sales team motivated.
5 We value _____ highly. That's why we don't give managers status symbols.
6 I'm not questioning the _____ of the idea. I just think it'll be tricky to actually implement, that's all.

Odd one out **3** Which word is the odd one out?

1 values	mindset	policy	beliefs
2 cost-conscious	thrifty	careful	pretentious
3 status	elite	rank	position
4 diverse	synonymous	uniform	cloned
5 discharge	rebuke	dismiss	sack
6 code	policy	rule	symbol

Writing practice: Formality in emails

Email ❶ Read the two emails below. Are the following statements true or false?

1 Emails always use informal language.
2 You should never send emails to people you don't know.
3 Emails are usually shorter than letters.
4 Very informal emails don't need opening and closing salutations.
5 Formal emails are very similar to formal letters.

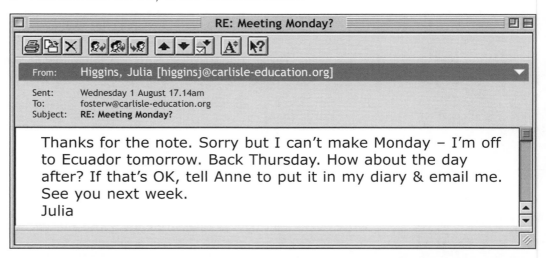

RE: Meeting Monday?

From: Higgins, Julia [higginsj@carlisle-education.org]

Sent: Wednesday 1 August 17.14am
To: fosterw@carlisle-education.org
Subject: **RE: Meeting Monday?**

Thanks for the note. Sorry but I can't make Monday – I'm off to Ecuador tomorrow. Back Thursday. How about the day after? If that's OK, tell Anne to put it in my diary & email me. See you next week.
Julia

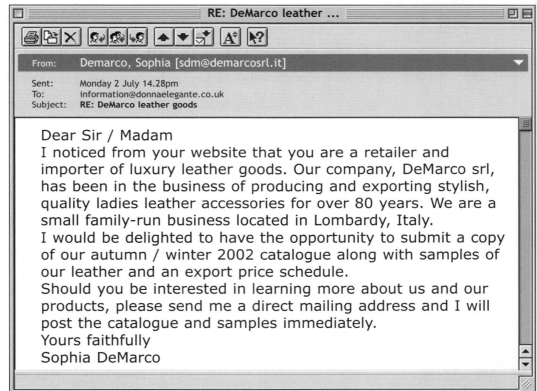

RE: DeMarco leather ...

From: Demarco, Sophia [sdm@demarcosrl.it]

Sent: Monday 2 July 14.28pm
To: information@donnaelegante.co.uk
Subject: **RE: DeMarco leather goods**

Dear Sir / Madam
I noticed from your website that you are a retailer and importer of luxury leather goods. Our company, DeMarco srl, has been in the business of producing and exporting stylish, quality ladies leather accessories for over 80 years. We are a small family-run business located in Lombardy, Italy.
I would be delighted to have the opportunity to submit a copy of our autumn / winter 2002 catalogue along with samples of our leather and an export price schedule.
Should you be interested in learning more about us and our products, please send me a direct mailing address and I will post the catalogue and samples immediately.
Yours faithfully
Sophia DeMarco

❷ Use the following tips to write a reply to each email.

• Respond with the same level of formality as in the original email.
• Email is usually a quick and short medium but when necessary, formal conventions must still be used.
• Use appropriate standard phrases (either formal or informal) for each reply.
• Use appropriate opening and closing salutations.

Ethics

Conditionals (real possibility)

Conditionals expressing real possibility have the following forms.

if + present tense, present tense / modal verb + infinitive
*If too many people **use** the system at once, it **runs** very slowly.*
*We**'ll risk** being fined if we **don't improve** our workplace safety.*

These conditionals are used in the following ways.

- to show cause and effect
  *If we **don't comply** with disposal regulations, we **get** fined.*

- to predict the effect of an action
  *There**'ll be** a scandal if the press **hear** about it.*

- to request action if something happens
  *Politely **refuse** to accept any gifts if they **offer** them to you.*

Note! *If* introduces a possible event. *When* introduces a definite event.

*Give her a warning **if** she's late. (She might be late.)*
*Let me know **when** she arrives. (She will definitely arrive.)*

Conditionals (hypothetical situations)

Conditionals expressing hypothetical situations have the following forms.

hypothetical situations in the present or future

if + past tense, *would / could / might* + infinitive
*If we **had** an ethical policy, we**'d / might attract** investment from ethical funds.*

hypothetical situations in the past

if + had + past participle, *would / could / might* + have + past participle
*We **could / might have stopped** the virus if we**'d had** better email security.*

Hypothetical conditionals are used in the following ways.

- to talk about hypothetical situations
  *If we **sued** our competitor, we**'d lose**. (= we're unlikely to sue)*
  *We **would have taken** action if we**'d known**. (= we didn't know)*

Note! The hypothetical present and future form of *be* is always *were*.

*I wouldn't launch the new product yet if I **were** you.*

Mixed conditionals

Some conditionals can mix past and present / future forms.

*If we**'d dealt** with the problem at the time, we **wouldn't be** in this mess.*
(past + present)

*If the plans **were stolen**, then we**'ll have to report** it to the police.*
(past + future)

Grammar practice

Real possibility ❶ Match the sentence halves.

1 If we issue passwords,	a) they receive legal protection.
2 If ethical funds perform well,	b) people will only forget them.
3 If we don't follow the disciplinary code,	c) we can't use the machine.
4 If we can't guarantee its safety,	d) we can't expect staff to follow them.
5 If we don't make the guidelines clear,	e) more people will be attracted to them.
6 If someone blows the whistle,	f) sacked employees can claim unfair dismissal.

Real and hypothetical possibility ❷ Complete the dialogue with the correct form of the verbs in brackets.

Janice   Peter, come in and take a seat. I'm afraid I've got some bad news. It looks like the Health and Safety Executive is going to ban the use of Petrotox in spray paints.

Peter   You're joking! It's one thing after another. What (¹we / use) _are we going to use_ then if we can't use Petrotox-based paints?

Janice   That's the question, isn't it? But if the HSE (²ban) _____ it, then we'll need to have a replacement ready. Any ideas?

Peter   Well, there are alternatives. But if we used them, then you do realise that our costs (³go) _____ up massively. How likely is the ban?

Janice   If the rumours (⁴be) _____ true, then it looks pretty certain, I'm afraid.

Peter   And what would happen if we just (⁵carry) _____ on using Petrotox anyway?

Janice   Come on Peter, you know that's not an option. If we (⁶do) _____, we'd be breaking the law.

Peter   How often does the HSE inspect us? They'd never know.

Janice   But you know as well as I do that if we (⁷carry) _____ on using a banned substance and they inspected us, we (⁸get) _____ a hefty fine and it (⁹be) _____ an absolute PR disaster.

Conditionals ❸ Complete the sentences with the correct form of the verbs in brackets.

1 Last year's harassment scandal (not / happen) _wouldn't have happened_ if we (appoint) ___'d appointed___ an ethics officer when we first discussed the idea.
2 If they (offer) _____ you any form of gifts while you're there on business, (not / accept) _____ them.
3 I (not / blow) _____ the whistle on the corporate racism that was going on if I (be) _____ him. It was a very brave thing to do.
4 If you (harass) _____ colleagues again in future, you (get) _____ a written warning.
5 I (not / want) _____ to work for a company if I (think) _____ they discriminated against anyone on account of their colour or race.
6 We (not / be) _____ in this situation now if we (issue) _____ a clear set of guidelines on discrimination.
7 If the accident (cause) _____ by defective machinery, then the company (face) _____ criminal proceedings.
8 The company (get) _____ a lot of 'fat cat' headlines in the newspapers if the board (award) _____ itself huge pay rises again this year.
9 I (not / invest) _____ in a company if I (find) _____ out that they (be) _____ any way involved in child labour.
10 He (not / able) _____ to steal the files if we (had) _____ proper information security – but it's too late now, of course.

Reading practice

1 Read the email and answer the questions on the opposite page.

From: Stokes, Natalie [natalie.fellows@ark-investments.co.uk]

Sent: Monday 2 July 2.17pm
To: Connolly, John
Subject: RE: green funds

John

Have you seen this month's IFA newsletter? I've copied it below in case you haven't. There's some really interesting stuff about green investment funds - just what we were talking about the other day. EIRIS has a directory we could get on, which would be great - if we could meet the criteria.

I reckon about 25% of our business would count as green so we might be able to make the minimum requirement with a bit of effort. A lot of our clients are asking about green funds but I'm not sure we could get enough of them to switch. What do you think? Should I send off for more details?

We'd also have to think about our investment strategy as we invest in all sorts of green firms at the moment. I think we'd have to decide which shade of green would suit us best. And what about the FTSE4Good? We could offer a fund that only invested in FTSE4Good companies. I'm sure it would be popular. What do you think?

Natalie

To: natalie.fellows@ark-investments.co.uk
From: news@theifa.co.uk
Date: 2 July 2001

The Independent Financial Advisor
Monthly Newsletter: July 2001

Dear Financial Advisor

You will no doubt be aware of the growing interest in ethical or 'green' investment. More and more clients are asking if there is any way of ensuring that their money is invested in companies that have no links to the tobacco or arms industry, show responsible employment practices and are committed to sustainable growth. There are currently 45 ethical investment funds in the UK managing over £2bn. In response to this trend, the London Stock Exchange (FTSE) will launch a green index at the end of the month called FTSE4Good. The new index has been developed with Unicef and the Ethical Investment Research Service (EIRIS) and firms must meet all three main entry criteria: environmental stability, relationship with stakeholders and support for human rights. Any fund managers using the index will pay a licence fee, which will be a donation to the international children's charity Unicef. For more information on FTSE4Good, go to www.ftse4good.com.

EIRIS has a national directory of ethical funds. If you wish to be included in this list, you will need to invest a minimum of £100,000 or 40 per cent of your business in green funds. Although all these funds exclude companies with any interests in tobacco, animal testing, nuclear power, oppressive regimes, gambling or pornography, they still range from 'dark green' funds, which have very strict exclusion rules and avoid oil companies and banks, to 'light green' funds that might invest in such companies provided they can prove a commitment to social and environmental issues. There is more information about the directory and qualification details at www.eiris.org.

1 What kind of company do you think John and Natalie work for?

    a) a publisher

    b) a financial services firm

    c) the London Stock Exchange

2 Where did the newsletter come from?

    a) an internal company newsletter

    b) a friend of Natalie's

    c) a trade magazine

3 Natalie thinks John will be interested in the newsletter because

    a) they were talking about ethical investments recently.

    b) he wants to invest his money in green funds.

    c) business is not going very well.

4 How many more customers would they need to qualify for the EIRIS directory?

    a) 15 per cent

    b) 25 per cent

    c) 40 per cent

5 What does Natalie mean by 'which shade of green would suit us'?

    a) how much money they should invest in green funds

    b) what percentage of their business should be in green funds

    c) what type of green funds they should invest in

6 Who launched the FTSE4Good?

    a) EIRIS

    b) The London Stock Exchange

    c) Unicef

7 The FTSE4Good index was launched because

    a) of the rapidly growing popularity of ethical investments.

    b) the charities saw a new opportunity to raise money.

    c) investors were showing no interest in green investments.

8 What must companies do to be listed on the FTSE4Good index?

    a) They must be one of the 100 largest companies in the UK.

    b) They must be listed on the EIRIS ethical funds directory.

    c) They must pass three types of strict ethical assessment.

Vocabulary **2** **Match the words from the text with their definitions.**

1	fund	a)	company's employees and shareholders
2	stakeholders	b)	money invested on behalf of several investors
3	sustainable growth	c)	something given for free
4	index	d)	list of companies whose shares are traded
5	criteria	e)	fair terms and conditions for employees
6	responsible employment practices	f)	organisation financed by gifts of money
7	donation	g)	governments with poor human rights records
8	charity	h)	list of companies
9	directory	i)	standards by which something is judged
10	oppressive regimes	j)	expansion that does not destroy resources

Vocabulary practice

Odd one out ❶ Which word does not go with the word in capital letters?

1 ETHICAL
   gossip   dilemma   behaviour   investment
2 OFFICIAL
   warning   policy   prejudice   guidelines
3 CORPORATE
   philanthropy   privacy   gift-giving   guidelines
4 LEGAL
   harassment   action   proceedings   compliance
5 SECURITY
   password   measures   procedures   perpetrator
6 ETHNIC
   minority   diversity   mismanagement   origin

Ethics ❷ Match the words then use them to complete the sentences below.

foul   blower
information   play
good   sector
industrial   correctness
political   practices
shady   causes
public   security
whistle   espionage

1 The company suspected ____*foul play*____ so hired a security expert to find out
   whether someone was giving confidential information to a competitor.
2 In the present atmosphere of _____, you have to be very careful what you
   say to colleagues at work. An inappropriate joke could be seen as harassment.
3 It takes a lot of courage to be a _____ . Powerful companies can put a lot of
   pressure on employees not to go to the press with stories of corporate wrong-doing.
4 The company donates a lot of money to _____. It also encourages staff to
   support charities by matching any private donations they give.
5 Hacking into another company's computers is a very rare form of _____.
   Computer hackers are normally individuals who target a company.
6 We're tightening up our _____ by issuing log-on passwords to all staff.
7 If they can't compete fairly, some companies resort to _____.
8 As there is no competition or profit-making in the _____, there are very few
   cases of industrial espionage.

Espionage ❸ Match the words with the definitions.

1 espionage   a) gaining unauthorised access to confidential computer data
2 investigation   b) spying to obtain secret information
3 bugging   c) secretly entering a place or organisation
4 infiltration   d) careful watch of someone suspected of doing wrong
5 hacking   e) collection and examination of evidence to find the truth
6 surveillance   f) fitting a secret microphone to a telephone or room

4 Match the verbs with the nouns then use them to complete the sentences.

produce   the law

take   an imitation

hack into   a grudge

issue   a system

bear   a fine

commit   legal action

comply with   passwords

pay   a crime

1 One of our competitors managed to *produce an imitation* of our secret recipe, which tasted exactly the same. That's when we suspected foul play.
2 Computer experts can _____ no matter how good its security is.
3 We're now under a lot of pressure to _____ on protecting whistle-blowers.
4 Most people think they don't _____ when they take stationery home from work for private use but in reality it's a form of theft.
5 We used to _____ but too many people forgot them and had to ring the IT department saying they were locked out of the computer system.
6 We knew someone was deleting important data from the server, so we asked all the managers if they had any employees that might _____ against the company.
7 When their main rival brought out a similar product, they decided to _____ on the grounds of an infringement of their patent.
8 The company had to _____ after being found guilty of paying for information from employees of one of their rivals.

Writing practice: linking

Formal report **1**   You have been asked to write a report on information security at your company. Use the notes below and the following tips to write a report of 200–250 words.

Aim – assess how good security is & propose ways of improving it

Findings – main points:

Use linkers of addition to list the main points

a) Everyone has access to the same central data – need to grade and restrict access to more sensitive info.

b) Disk drives can be used to copy data & take it out of the building – why not disable disk drives so people can't copy files? They can forward files to each other internally using the system. Problem with taking work home?   *State the possible drawbacks of an idea - use linkers*

c) No-one has log-in codes so no record of who's using the system – definitely need to assign log-on codes to keep track of who's accessing what. People forgetting passwords?

Conclusion – security not very good & needs tightening a lot.

Use sequencers to list action points

Recommendations:

1) Grade & restrict access to sensitive information to managers only.

2) Must assign log-on codes to all employees.

3) Disable disk drives – only let certain PAs copy files to take home.

Ethics

Globalisation

Reported speech

The following tense and time changes can be used in reported speech.

'They're selling well now.'	She said (that) they were selling well then.
'I saw them yesterday.'	She said (that) she'd seen them the day before.
'We bought it a year ago.'	He said (that) they'd bought it a year before.
'I haven't seen the brochure.'	She said (that) she hadn't seen the brochure.
'I'll call you this week.'	He said (that) he'd call me that week.
'We're leaving tomorrow.'	They said (that) they were leaving the next day.

Verbs used to report speech can be followed by

- the tense used by the speaker
  She **said** (that) the brand **isn't** very well-known in Sweden.

- a tense change (admit, agree, complain, explain, promise, say)
  She **explained** (that) the French **saw** yoghurt as a health food.

- an infinitive (agree, ask, decide, demand, offer, promise, refuse, want)
  We **decided to localise** all the packaging.

- a gerund (admit, deny, mention, report)
  He didn't **mention meeting** Luisa at the conference.

- an object + infinitive (advise, ask, instruct, invite, remind, tell, warn)
  We **advised them to adapt** the product to the local market.

Note! In reported questions, the subject and verb are not inverted. There is no auxiliary verb *do*.

She **asked** me **where the contract was**.
They **asked** us **whether the goods had arrived** on time.

The verbs *suggest, recommend* and *advise* are never followed immediately by *to*. They are often followed by *-ing* or *that*.

I suggest ~~to look~~ into the possibility of a joint venture.
I suggest looking into the possibility of a joint venture.
I suggest (that) you look into the possibility of a joint venture.

Inversion

The verb and subject are inverted in the following situations.

- after negative sentence openers
  Never have we seen such terrible market conditions.
  On no account should we risk the quality of our product.
  No sooner had we built the new plant **than** the market collapsed.
  Not only does it sell in Germany **but also** in Austria. (note auxiliary verb do)
  Under no circumstances will we renegotiate the agreed delivery dates.

- after *only, rarely, little*
  Only in the Far East **can we produce** them so quickly.
  Rarely does changing suppliers result in good quality.
  Little did I know our competitors already had a factory there.

Grammar practice

Reported speech ① Rewrite the sentences using reported speech.

1 We've been doing business in Hong Kong since 1984.
   She said that _they'd been doing business in Hong Kong since 1984._

2 Have you sent the brochures yet?
   He asked me _____

3 Are you going to the trade convention in Cancun?
   She asked me _____

4 When did you arrive in Bahrain?
   She asked me _____

5 We're negotiating a deal with a local distributor in Cracow.
   He admitted that _____

6 We'll dispatch your order tomorrow.
   She promised that _____

Summarising ② Use the following reporting verbs to summarise the report extracts below.

~~admit~~   agree   recommend   refuse   warn

1 Faced with an investigation, the company submitted files showing it had been using a banned chemical.

2 Stone & Co. would be ill-advised to contest the legal action as the weight of evidence is heavily against the company.

3 Despite evidence to the contrary, the company was unwilling to accept any charges of racial discrimination.

4 We therefore strongly advise the company to appoint an ethics officer and draw up an official code of ethics.

5 In conclusion, Mr Giddins was dismissed according to the disciplinary code and has no grounds for unfair dismissal.

1 The company _admitted using a_ _banned chemical._

2 The report _____
   _____

3 The company _____
   _____

4 The report _____
   _____

5 The report _____
   _____

Inversion ③ Use the following sentence openers to rewrite the statements below.

~~Not only~~   No sooner   On no account   Little   Never   Only

1 We've got problems in both Argentina and Brazil.
   Not only do we have problems in Argentina, but also in Brazil.

2 We'd just found a joint venture partner and then they went bankrupt!
   _____

3 I had no idea that they were selling on the black market for $10 each.
   _____

4 We can reduce the features, but there's no way we're going to compromise on quality.
   _____

5 I've never experienced such a dramatic rise and fall in a company's fortunes.
   _____

6 We can only sell our products in markets where English is spoken.
   _____

Reading practice

1 Match each of the statements on the opposite page with one of the letters below.

Letters to the editor

Tuesday's editorial column on the violent anti-globalisation protests at the recent International Monetary Fund (IMF) meeting in Seattle produced a large response from our readers. Here is a selection showing the range of opinions we received.

Dear Sir

Globalisation is nothing new – in fact it's as old as civilisation itself. From the days of the Roman Empire, economic powers have always looked to increase their wealth through trade. This process has always brought different cultures into contact, with both sides learning new ideas and customs from each other. If trade didn't benefit both parties, it wouldn't happen, so I don't believe it's true that globalisation today is only benefiting rich western countries such as the USA. Globalisation is all about increasing wealth and the choice of goods for everyone. Technology is making this easier and bringing the world and its economies closer together, which can only be a good thing in my opinion. Increased trade leads to information exchange and an increased understanding of other cultures. The world's largest economic sector - tourism - is a result of this spread of information and interest in other cultures. Globalisation has also helped to spread democracy, improve human rights and set environmental standards in many countries that look to participate in the global marketplace.

John, Washington DC (by email)

Dear Sir

The recent anti-globalisation protests in Seattle show that an increasingly large and varied group of people are very concerned about the effects of liberalised world trade. Anti-poverty campaigners, environmentalists, trade unions and human rights activists from all over the world are concerned that:
1) globalisation widens the economic gap between the world's richest and poorest countries. The latest World Bank report states the gap between the average income in the richest and poorest 20 countries has doubled in the past 40 years.
2) national cultures are under threat from satellite TV, mass tourism and multinationals selling the same goods in every country. In French cinemas, most films are now made in Hollywood.
3) multinationals are becoming more powerful than elected governments. A large US energy company recently forced the state of California to legalise a chemical used in petrol that the California state government had banned for health reasons. At the current World Trade talks, multinationals are looking to secure the same powers over foreign national governments.
4) multinationals serve only their shareholders and are interested in huge profits only – not in environmental sustainability - especially in overseas markets. If these companies are more powerful than governments, who can protect our environment?

Martina, Prague

Dear Sir

I recently took part in a one-day strike in protest at our government's economic reforms that will allow multinationals to enter the country. I do not believe that liberalisation is the only way to achieve efficiency. For many years, India has benefited from efficient industries secured by protection from outside competition - as did countries such as Germany and Japan. Our large semi-skilled workforce and strengths in information technology should place India in a good position to benefit from globalisation and many Indians want to participate in the revolution – but at what cost? Once these foreign multinationals become established in the country, can the government ensure that they will operate in the interests of the millions living in poverty and not just those with money to buy their goods?

Sourav Gupta, Mombai (by email)

1) Mass tourism is a good thing. *John, Washington DC*
2) Globalisation is a danger to cultural variety in different countries.
3) His or her country will probably benefit economically from globalisation.
4) Free world trade benefits all countries.
5) Foreign competition does not improve domestic industrial performance.
6) Globalisation strengthens democratic and human rights.
7) Opposition to globalisation is growing stronger and stronger.
8) Multinationals help to protect the environment.

2 Read the letters again and answer the questions.

1 What event took place in Seattle recently?
2 What happened at this event?
3 Which anti-globalisation groups were in Seattle?
4 What other act of protest is mentioned in the letters?
5 What does Martina see as the main threats to national culture?
6 Why does Sourav think India might benefit from globalisation?

3 Read the letters again and complete the table with the possible opportunities and threats posed by globalisation.

	opportunities	threats
wealth	*increased wealth for everyone*	*the rich get richer while the poor get poorer*
culture		
the environment		
the role of governments		
range of products		
film / television		
mass tourism		

Vocabulary **4** Match the words from the text with their definitions.

1 globalisation   a) change in a country's business laws and practices
2 democracy   b) internationalisation of markets and companies
3 anti-poverty campaigner   c) ability to maintain something without damaging it
4 mass tourism   d) removal of legal barriers to free trade
5 multinational   e) business of providing holidays for lots of people
6 sustainability   f) system of government based on election by the public
7 economic reform   g) person who fights for the rights of the world's poor
8 liberalisation   h) large company with offices in many different countries

Vocabulary practice

Global
sourcing

1 Complete the word diagram with the following words.

~~increased profits~~   negative publicity   strategic alliance   lower labour costs
lower quality   buying the market   competitive advantage
shorter time to market   cultural differences   currency exchange fluctuations
global presence   access to markets   full ownership

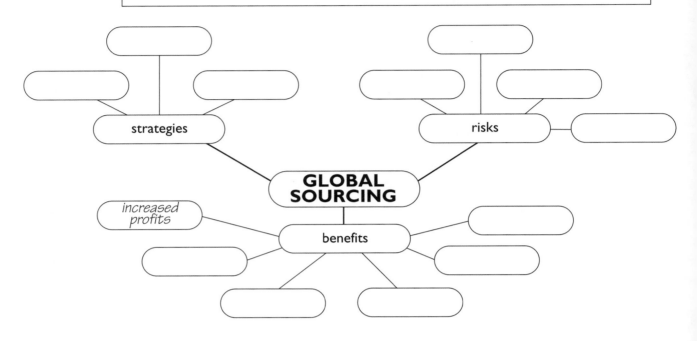

2 Complete the sentences with the following words.

~~to~~   with   up   into   in   to   for   of

1 All of our products conform __to__ EU safety regulations.
2 By centralising production at our Slovakia plant, we've been able to realise substantial economies _____ scale.
3 Because we localise our products, overseas customers are more able to identify _____ them.
4 We weighed _____ all the factors and decided to look for a joint venture partner.
5 I think the main catalyst _____ change was the creation of the single European currency.
6 Our first plant there was a big risk as we had little expertise _____ the region.
7 After problems with quality, we decided to shift _____ a long-term supplier relationship strategy and invested in equipment and training for our main supplier.
8 The aggressive growth strategy saw us expand _____ several new territories.

3 Match the verbs with the nouns.

1 economic   a) presence
2 cultural   b) necessity
3 global   c) process
4 supply   d) criteria
5 key   e) stereotype
6 bidding   f) chain
7 tight   g) deadlines

Writing practice: Mixed practice

❶ You work for QuayWest, a leisurewear retailer. Read the email, letter and notes below, which have been sent to you by colleagues and a customer. Write suitable replies. Remember the following.

- Who is the reader? What level of formality is appropriate?
- How long should each reply be?
- How should each reply be organised?
- What standard phrases will be useful?
- Check each reply for errors.

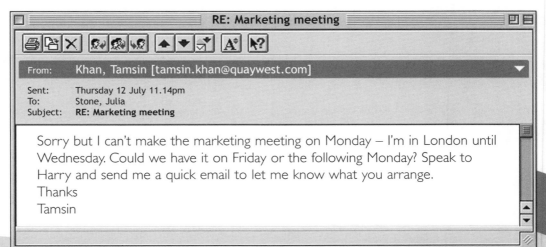

RE: Marketing meeting

From: Khan, Tamsin [tamsin.khan@quaywest.com]

Sent: Thursday 12 July 11.14pm
To: Stone, Julia
Subject: **RE: Marketing meeting**

Sorry but I can't make the marketing meeting on Monday – I'm in London until Wednesday. Could we have it on Friday or the following Monday? Speak to Harry and send me a quick email to let me know what you arrange.
Thanks
Tamsin

Re: Marketing meeting
Can't make meeting with Tamsin on Friday I'm afraid but following Monday is OK. What time? Email me.
Harry

---

1 – Yes, order 300 pairs.
2 – No, cancel orange jackets.
3 – White T-shirts, order 100 Extra large, 300 Large, 300 Medium & 200 Small.
Delivery date is 1 March. Apologise for mistake.

Dear Ms Harrison

Re: Your order RF20078/01

Thank you very much for the above-mentioned order, which received last week. We are very grateful for your business and complete the order on time and to your full satisfaction.

In order to do this, we will need you to answer the following que

1. Article HX02/0240 ladies jeans. You have ordered 250 pairs. O discount schedule would give you an extra 3% for an order of 30 pairs. Would you like to increase the quantity to 300?
2. Article HX02/0081 boys jackets. We no longer produce these in orange. Would you like these in an alternative colour?
3. Article HX02/0009 white T-shirts. You didn't state the sizes you would like for these articles. What sizes and how many of each would you like?

Could you also confirm the deadline for this order? At our last meeting we noted a delivery date of 1 March. However, your order stated 1 February. This date would prove very difficult for us to achieve and was a great surprise to us. Please confirm the correct date as soon as possible.

I look forward to hearing from you soon in order that we may begin work on your order without delay.

Yours sincerely

Charlie Li

Charlie Li
Sales Executive
Hai Xin Group

Here are last month's weekly production figures, showing the previous month's figures as well. Could you do a short report summarising the figures and email it to me to forward to the MD? Don't forget to mention the supply problems we had at the start of April and the effect the new machinery started to have in May – 91,320 units is a factory record after all!

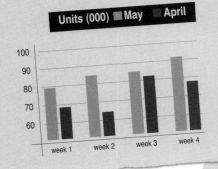

Units (000) ■ May ■ April

Review unit 2 (5–8)

Grammar

① Complete the presentation with appropriate reference words.

Good morning, ladies and gentlemen, and thank you very much for coming to ¹_____ training session. My name is Adam Lukic and today I'm going to discuss cultural differences and the effect they can have on people ²_____ as yourselves when working abroad. I'll begin by taking a brief look at typical responses to being alone in a foreign environment and the limitations of ³_____ responses. We'll then go on to discuss how value systems can differ and the benefits of accepting ⁴_____ as a simple fact of life. ⁵_____ will include a look at our own values and how ⁶_____ could seem strange and illogical to others.

So, let's begin with two extreme, but very typical, responses to working abroad, which we call the 'expat syndrome' and 'going native'. ⁷_____ is when the person totally rejects the new culture, whereas ⁸_____ is when the person totally embraces the new culture to the point where they are no longer interested in their own culture. Now, although it's clear that neither of ⁹_____ extremes is healthy, anyone who thinks ¹⁰_____ could never happen to them underestimates the disorientating effect being alone in a foreign country can have.

The people who fall into the 'expat syndrome' category are ¹¹_____ who make no attempt to learn the local language, only socialise with their own nationals, take no interest in social and political events and refuse to participate in the traditions and customs of the host country. ¹²_____ attitude is very much the result of a mindset that sees an overseas posting as nothing more than a temporary inconvenience which has no long-term benefits apart from possible career advancement. For many people posted overseas, ¹³_____ is certainly the case.

On the other hand, we have ¹⁴_____ who 'go native'. For many people, the first weeks of an overseas posting are very exciting. Everything is new and fascinating - an effect we call the 'honeymoon period'. For most, ¹⁵_____ wears off after a few weeks. But for some, it doesn't. They become so attracted to the new culture that they compare it favourably to their own. It's not hard to imagine the problems this causes when they complete their posting and return to their own country.

2 Complete the dialogue with the correct gerund or infinitive forms.

Karl   Ah, Sarah. I've got some exciting news for you.

Sarah Oh, what's that?

Karl   Well, do you remember (¹see) _____ those Koreans a few months ago? Well, I forgot (²mention) _____ that they were officials from the Korean government, who were here to negotiate a contract (³supply) _____ official merchandise for the 2002 World Cup. Well, the negotiations went well and we've just managed (⁴close) _____ the deal.

Sarah That's great.

Karl   It's a huge contract. It won't be easy (⁵meet) _____ deadlines on top of our other orders, but we decided (⁶accept) _____ their terms and not risk (⁷lose) _____ the whole thing.

Sarah No, there's no point in (⁸risk) _____ the whole contract over order numbers. But do we have enough capacity (⁹produce) _____ the agreed volumes?

Karl   Well, Peter and I worked out that we'll need (¹⁰increase) _____ capacity by about 20 per cent over the next eight months.

Sarah We can't do that without (¹¹recruit) _____ more workers.

Karl   I know and that's why I need (¹²talk) _____ to you. We're planning (¹³install) _____ a fourth production line.

Sarah A fourth line? We'll need (¹⁴man) _____ it, of course. (¹⁵train) _____ will be an issue as well. A new production line will mean new machinery, which people will have to learn to use. Not to mention (¹⁶have) _____ (¹⁷train) _____ new staff as well. That's all going to take time, you know.

Karl   I know. That's why we'd like you to make a start (¹⁸research) _____ all these issues straight away. You can start by (¹⁹advertise) _____ for new staff right away, while you're putting a report together.

Sarah Right. OK. I'll make a start. It's going to be a lot of work though.

Karl   I warned you (²⁰not / book) _____ any holidays this year, didn't I?

3 Complete the report extract with the active or passive form of the verbs in brackets.

A recent ethical audit, which (¹carry) _____ out in May, showed that the company's operations included several practices that (²might / judge) _____ as unethical by shareholders and the general public. It (³find) _____ that the company employed no workers from ethnic minorities. Moreover, many of the company's products (⁴sourced) _____ from overseas markets where cheap labour, including child labour, (⁵employ) _____. Although there is no evidence of the company using such labour, it (⁶could / see) _____ to indirectly support its use. Several newspaper stories (⁷publish) _____ recently showing how cheaply top brands (⁸produce) _____ on the subcontinent compared with the premium prices at which they (⁹sold) _____ in Europe. As a well-known manufacturer of branded leisurewear with suppliers who (¹⁰locate) _____ on the subcontinent, we (¹¹could / easily / put) _____ into this category by national newspapers and consequently the public. Needless to say that investor attitudes (¹²might / also / affect) _____ if this (¹³happen) _____ in the future. It is clear that action needs (¹⁴take) _____ to avoid such negative publicity. It (¹⁵recommend) _____ therefore that the company review its employment policies and commission a new ethical audit with a view to publishing it as part of a campaign to promote the company's ethical credentials.

4 **Which of the three options would not complete each sentence?**

1 _____ I use your phone, please?
   a) May b) Will c) Can

2 We _____ reach agreement at the last meeting.
   a) weren't able to b) wouldn't c) couldn't

3 You _____ use a mobile phone during the flight.
   a) don't have to b) mustn't c) shouldn't

4 It _____ be a difficult year ahead with the economy performing as badly as it is.
   a) 'll b) 's going to c) shall

5 You _____ have a local sponsor before you can go there on business.
   a) will b) have to c) must

6 What _____ do about it?
   a) will you b) may you c) are you going to

7 They _____ re-arrange the visit for July. We don't know yet.
   a) might b) 'll c) may

8 _____ I phone Reception and get them to bring some room service up?
   a) Should b) Shall c) Will

9 Don't try to lift that case. It's too heavy. I _____ do it.
   a) 'll b) can c) must

10 With all the extra security, we _____ check in at least two hours before the flight.
   a) may b) have to c) should

11 We _____ adapt the product to the African market.
   a) might b) 're going to c) shall

12 We _____ get a taxi back to the hotel. It won't be very expensive from here.
   a) could b) shall c) should

13 _____ you pass me those handouts, please?
   a) Would b) May c) Could

14 If Zoe doesn't arrive soon, I _____ ring her on that phone in the corner.
   a) would b) 'll c) can

15 We _____ have any cultural awareness training before we left for China.
   a) weren't allowed to b) couldn't c) may not

5 **Use the verbs in the box to report the following sentences.**

admit
invite
deny
advise
suggest
remind
ask
warn
complain
promise

1 I'm afraid it was me who accidentally sent them the sales figures.
   _____

2 Why don't we advertise on the internet?
   _____

3 Don't use my office email address because my boss sometimes checks it.
   _____

4 Would you be available to attend an interview on 23 October at 10 am?
   _____

5 Don't worry. I won't tell anyone that you're looking for a new job.
   _____

6 Have you got any experience of working with html?
   _____

7 I didn't lie on my CV. It was a genuine mistake.
   _____

8 If I were you, I'd phone up and ask to speak to the HR Officer.
   _____

9 Don't forget to put some information about hobbies on your CV.
   _____

10 There are too many applications. How am I going to read them all before tomorrow?
   _____

6 Complete the sentences with the correct conditional form.

1 If we (*not / look*) _____ to expand soon, we (*fall*) _____ behind our competitors within three years.

2 If their European outlets (*not / lose*) _____ so much money, then they (*not / close*) _____ them down last year.

3 We (*not / be*) _____ in a mess now if we (*secure*) _____ better terms at the original negotiations.

4 If there (*be*) _____ any problems at customs, (*call*) _____ me.

5 This recession (*affect*) _____ us more if we (*not / have*) _____ as many diversified businesses as we do.

6 If the goods (*lose*) _____ in transit, then we (*have*) _____ to send them a replacement order. But I want proof first that that's what happened.

7 The unions (*call*) _____ a strike if the merger (*go*) _____ ahead as looks likely.

8 If sales (*continue*) _____ to grow as they are, we (*beat*) _____ our all-time 12-month sales record by the end of the year.

9 They (*not / license*) _____ local production if it (*not / be*) _____ for all the black market copies that were being sold anyway.

10 (*not / let*) _____ Jack see the report before I (*see*) _____ it.

11 If we (*find*) _____ the right partner, we (*pursue*) _____ a joint venture strategy, but we just couldn't find one.

12 I (*adapt*) _____ the product to the market if I (*be*) _____ you.

13 If the goods (*ship*) _____ on Tuesday, they (*arrive*) _____ by the fifteenth of next month.

14 If the contract (*sign*) _____ last year, we (*all / make*) _____ a lot of money right now. We missed a great opportunity.

15 If the goods (*not / leave*) _____ Rotterdam until last Monday, then I doubt they (*arrive*) _____ yet.

7 Use the negative sentence openers to rewrite the following sentences.

1 They'd just completed the merger and then they sacked all the management.
No sooner _____.

2 I'm sorry but we cannot accept the terms of the deal.
Under no circumstances _____.

3 Whatever you do, don't sign the contract until I get there.
On no account _____.

4 The company has never made such profits before.
Never _____.

5 My plane was delayed because of a bomb scare at the airport.
Little did I know _____.

6 You can only really understand another culture when you live in the country.
Only _____.

7 They don't work late and they don't work weekends either.
Not only _____.

8 It's not often that you meet a British person who speaks Japanese so well.
Rarely _____.

9 We'll only sign the contract after it's been translated into French.
Only _____.

10 Sending people abroad without cultural awareness training is out of the question.
On no account _____.

Vocabulary

Complete each sentence with the correct option.

1 Salary is a not necessarily the greatest factor in job _____.
   a) contentment   b) satisfaction   c) enrichment
2 _____ is an important attribute at IKEA. We don't tolerate arrogance.
   a) vitality   b) thrift   c) humility
3 Many companies are now more sensitive to the dangers of corporate _____.
   a) gift-giving   b) gift exchange   c) gift swapping
4 We have a strategic _____ in Germany, so we distribute through our partner.
   a) venture   b) friendship   c) alliance
5 Once a headhunter is instructed, he receives a _____ for his services.
   a) retainer   b) proportion   c) remuneration
6 The company values are officially expressed through its _____ statement.
   a) beliefs   b) objective   c) mission
7 There are many _____ about corporate spies, but I doubt they are true.
   a) urban legends   b) investigations   c) accusations
8 Companies that island _____ in the hope of cutting costs risk quality.
   a) jump   b) leap   c) hop
9 The _____ will receive an official job offer within about three weeks.
   a) trainee   b) interviewee   c) appointee
10 The company is strict about staff complying with the official dress _____.
   a) sense   b) code   c) obligation
11 A competitor _____ our sales team and got a lot of inside information.
   a) perpetrated   b) surveyed   c) infiltrated
12 Advertising that _____ a national stereotype can be very successful.
   a) portrays   b) reveals   c) creates
13 The benefits package was one of the main _____ for choosing this job.
   a) motivations   b) criteria   c) contributions
14 The _____ has to be good so we don't compete against our own products.
   a) diversity   b) status   c) positioning
15 No computer system is completely safe from _____.
   a) hacking   b) surveillance   c) violation
16 The racial discrimination case created a lot of bad _____ for the company.
   a) circumstance   b) publicity   c) coverage
17 Headhunters scan online _____ to get the names of contributors.
   a) news rooms   b) news pages   c) newsgroups
18 Our product was so successful that competitors started producing _____.
   a) clones   b) tributes   c) copyrights
19 The manager had to leave when he was found guilty of _____.
   a) embarrassment   b) compliance   c) harassment
20 Low interest rates were a _____ for a wave of investment in new machinery.
   a) criteria   b) cause   c) catalyst
21 We have a job _____ policy so everyone gains experience of different jobs.
   a) rotation   b) opportunities   c) appraisal
22 We believe in equality so managers don't have _____ such as company cars.
   a) valuables   b) status symbols   c) pretentions
23 According to shop floor _____, we're going to be sold to our main rival.
   a) morale   b) evidence   c) gossip
24 The euro cuts costs by ending currency _____ amongst Eurozone countries.
   a) overheads   b) complexity   c) exchange risk
25 Praise is a key _____ factor, but different cultures approach it differently.
   a) appraisal   b) motivational   c) behavioural
26 We have several new managerial _____ to improve team spirit.
   a) initiatives   b) policies   c) codes

27　We need to _____ a system for tracking who accesses the data.
　　a) suspect　　　　　b) devise　　　　　　c) hack
28　A high percentage of the goods were _____ and had to be returned.
　　a) defective　　　　b) desirable　　　　　c) deducted
29　A headhunter has started an executive _____ for our new CEO.
　　a) hunt　　　　　　b) search　　　　　　c) appointment
30　We fell well short of our targets, which were too _____ to begin with.
　　a) pretentious　　　b) imposing　　　　　c) optimistic
31　Legal _____ is a major ethical issue for most of the CEOs interviewed.
　　a) compatibility　　b) contribution　　　c) compliance
32　We're using a recruitment agency as well as our own _____ process.
　　a) selection　　　　b) search　　　　　　c) scanning
33　One culture's customs and traditions are just as _____ as another's.
　　a) vivid　　　　　　b) valid　　　　　　c) vital
34　They were using banned chemicals until a _____ went to the press.
　　a) whizzkid　　　　b) whistle-blower　　c) informer
35　For many people German engineering is _____ with high quality.
　　a) equal　　　　　　b) synonymous　　　c) uniform
36　In order to improve information security, we're going to _____ passwords.
　　a) issue　　　　　　b) access　　　　　　c) log on
37　Lucy received an official _____ for continued bad time-keeping.
　　a) threat　　　　　b) code　　　　　　c) warning
38　Using cheap labour could have negative PR _____ for the company.
　　a) circumstances　　b) fluctuations　　　c) implications
39　We put the specifications on the web and invited _____ to submit tenders.
　　a) purchasers　　　b) vendors　　　　　c) alliances
40　A headhunter must be very _____ when approaching possible candidates.
　　a) submissive　　　b) extensive　　　　c) discreet
41　It's difficult to change the _____ of a whole department when morale is low.
　　a) values　　　　　b) mindset　　　　　c) consciousness
42　When a lot of illegal copies started turning up, we began to suspect _____.
　　a) a grudge　　　　b) foul play　　　　　c) a whistle-blower
43　We need to speed up production and reduce our _____ to market.
　　a) time　　　　　　b) duration　　　　　c) period
44　We're a small company so we aim for a high market share of _____ markets.
　　a) niche　　　　　　b) saturated　　　　　c) global
45　We're famous for our _____. Not a cent is wasted at this company.
　　a) humility　　　　b) philanthropy　　　c) thrift
46　Using environmentally unsustainable materials would go against our _____.
　　a) principals　　　b) priorities　　　　c) principles
47　With today's political _____ in the office, you have to watch what you say.
　　a) espionage　　　b) correctness　　　c) privacy
48　The discrimination was judged a personal _____ and not a company policy.
　　a) prejudice　　　　b) paranoia　　　　　c) persuasion
49　Managers were presented with ethical _____ and asked for solutions.
　　a) circumstances　　b) dilemmas　　　　c) visions
50　After several attacks on staff, they reviewed their security _____.
　　a) behaviour　　　b) measures　　　　　c) campaign

Verb lists

Verbs followed by -ing

admit	enjoy	recommend
appreciate	finish	report
avoid	go	resist
carry on	imagine	risk
celebrate	involve	suggest
commence	keep	
consider	mention	
continue	mind	
delay	miss	
deny	postpone	
dislike	practise	

Phrases followed by -ing

be used to	it's no good	make a start
can't help	it's no use	object to
can't stand	look forward to	there's no point

Verbs followed by an infinitive

afford	fight	prepare
agree	hesitate	promise
aim	hope	prove
appear	intend	refuse
arrange	learn	seem
ask	manage	tend
choose	mean	threaten
decide	neglect	wait
demand	need	want
expect	offer	wish
fail	plan	

Verbs followed by object + infinitive

advise someone (not) to ...
allow someone (not) to ...
ask someone (not) to ...
encourage someone (not) to ...
expect someone (not) to ...
get someone (not) to ...
instruct someone (not) to ...
invite someone (not) to ...
leave someone (not) to ...
order someone (not) to ...
persuade someone (not) to ...
recommend someone (not) to ...
remind someone (not) to ...
tell someone (not) to ...
warn someone (not) to ...

Verbs followed by -ing or infinitive

With little /no difference in meaning

attempt	hate	prefer
begin	like	start
continue	love	try

With some difference in meaning

- regret
  (-ing refers to a past action)
  I **regret not telling** you about the problem earlier.
  (an infinitive introduces bad news)
  We **regret to tell** you we cannot replace the goods.

- remember / forget
  (-ing refers to a past action)
  Do you **remember meeting** Jessica last year?
  (an infinitive refers to a future action)
  Remember to take your passport, won't you?

Verbs followed by that

add	explain	report
admit	fear	reveal
agree	feel	say
announce	insist	state
argue	mention	suggest
claim	promise	tell
complain	propose	think
confirm	remark	threaten
decide	remember	understand
deny	repeat	warn

Verbs of suggesting

Suggest, recommend and *advise* are never followed immediately by *to*. They are often followed by *-ing* or *that*.

I suggest to meet at about 7.30 pm.
I suggest meeting at 7.30 pm.
I suggest (that) we meet at 7.30 pm.

Answer key (Units 1–8)

Unit 1: Organisation
Grammar practice

1
2 doesn't arrive
3 are you staying
4 feel
5 do you report
6 don't need
7 doesn't start
8 'm seeing

2
2 ran
3 asked
4 've done
5 haven't implemented
6 came
7 have we done
8 've started
9 haven't managed
10 've had
11 's been
12 didn't you explain
13 asked
14 came
15 Have you spoken
16 spoke
17 said
18 would

3
2 read
3 been running
4 filled
5 been working
6 been waiting
7 gone
8 been working

Reading practice

1 Order: a, h, b, e, d, g, f, c

2
2 h
3 b
4 e
5 d
6 g
7 f
8 c

3
1 a
2 c
3 c
4 a
5 b
6 b

4
2 e
3 f
4 a
5 d
6 c

Vocabulary practice

1
2 assignment
3 response
4 assessment
5 balance
6 motivation
7 co-ordination
8 allocation
9 collaboration

2
2 business units
3 communication channels
4 company structure
5 flexible working
6 online support
7 competitive advantage
8 operating processes

3
2 a
3 f
4 e
5 d
6 c

Writing practice

1 See sample answer on page 75.

Unit 2: Mergers
Grammar practice

1
2 The offer price, which is $18 a share, was confirmed yesterday.
3 They've increased the original offer (which / that) they made last week.
4 The merger, which hasn't been approved yet, will make them the biggest bank in the UK.
5 They'll need the approval of private shareholders, who own 35% of the company.
6 Shareholders have lost faith in the board, whose expansion strategy has lost £800m.
7 The merger was masterminded by Luc Van der Saar, to whom all credit should go.
8 The company sold the web TV subsidiary (which / that) it bought two years ago.
9 After the merger they closed 64 retail outlets which / that were in similar locations.
10 We're having problems integrating two management styles which / that are very different.

2
2 erratic
3 suddenly
4 quickly
5 marked
6 slightly
7 reasonably
8 stable
9 sharply
10 strong
11 steadily

Reading practice

1 c

2
1 AOL ($163bn)
2 Time Warner (TV news and entertainment channels plus many publications)
3 AOL (majority stake)
4 They went up. (AOL +19%, Time Warner +12%.)
5 AOL needed content, whereas Time Warner wanted internet distribution for its content.
6 Online experience and 20 million subscribers.
7 Increase market share (CompuServe) and knowledge base (Netscape).
8 Lack of experience and strategy disagreements.
9 Skills, expertise and a profitable TV news channel.
10 Regulatory review. (Monopolies Commission)

❸ 2 c   4 a
3 d   5 e

❹ 2 Both are news channels owned by Time Warner.
3 Time Warner owns the Cartoon Network.
4 AOL owns Netscape.
5 Disney owns ABC.
6 AOL Time Warner is a competitor of Disney.

❺ 2 i   7 c
3 f   8 e
4 h   9 d
5 j   10 g
6 a

❻ 2 Although   4 as well as
3 while   5 however

Vocabulary practice

❶ 2 rollercoaster ride / fluctuate
3 go through the roof / soar
6 slide / fall steadily
5 reach a high / peak
6 cooling of enthusiasm / fall off

❷ 2 e   6 c
3 h   7 d
4 g   8 a
5 f

❸ 2 demerger   5 diversify
3 sell-off   6 merge
4 dividends

❹ advantages   problems
economies of scale   destabilisation
synergies   duplicated functions
diversification   redundancies
increased revenue

2 diversification
3 integration of cultures
4 synergies
5 redundancies
6 economies of scale
7 increased revenue
8 duplicated functions
9 destabilisation

Writing practice

❶ See sample answer on page 75.

Unit 3: Selling
Grammar practice

❶ 2 after   5 before
3 while   6 as soon as
4 until

❷ 2 'll read, 'm waiting
3 Don't forget, get
4 've finished, 'll take
5 won't arrange, confirm / 've confirmed
6 'll give, leave
7 'm going to play, 'm visiting
8 'll pick, 've had

❸ 2 the   12 the
3 the   13 a
4 a   14 an
5 Ø   15 the
6 the   16 Ø
7 Ø   17 Ø
8 Ø   18 the
9 the   19 a
10 Ø   20 the
11 Ø / the

Reading practice

❶ c

❷ 1 Home improvement retailer.
2 More potential for growth than in Europe.
3 58 stores operating by 2005.
4 Rising living standards and construction boom.
5 Adaptation of product lines (e.g. no garden furniture and wallpaper).

❸ 1 F (it trades under its B&Q brand)
2 F (there are 550 *Kingfisher* stores worldwide)
3 F (*one* of Europe's leading electrical retailers)
4 F (Paris-based)
5 F (China in 1995)
6 F (58 stores refers to its growth target for 2005)
7 F (rising living standards are making DIY popular)
8 T (government programmes building suburbs)
9 F (no garden centres or wallpaper in China)
10 T (most Chinese live in small apartments)

❹ 2 in France
3 the Asia-Pacific region
4 stores operating in the Asia-Pacific region
5 the Yangpu megastore
6 general growth in Asia for B&Q
7 kitchen and bathroom fittings
8 stores

❺ 2 e   4 f   6 a
3 d   5 c

6
2 h   6 a
3 f   7 c
4 e   8 d
5 g

Vocabulary practice

1
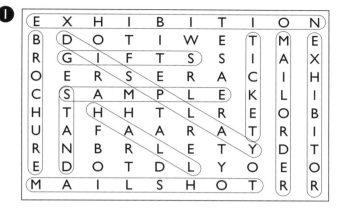

2
2 trade literature   5 entry strategy
3 intense negotiations   6 commercial interests
4 independent retailers

Writing practice

1 See sample answer on page 76.

Unit 4: Technology
Grammar practice

1
1 c   4 a
2 b   5 c
3 b   6 a

2
2 're all going
3 're cutting
4 won't / isn't going to be
5 will / are going to be
6 might not / won't be able to
7 'll / 's going to send
8 go
9 'll / 'm going to have to
10 won't / isn't going to be
11 Isn't she doing

3
2 'll have reached   5 will be announcing
3 won't be making   6 'll have spent
4 Will you have finished

Reading practice

1
1 b   4 c
2 c   5 b
3 b   6 a

2
2 a   5 g   8 d
3 h   6 e
4 f   7 c

3 the companies
European telecoms sector
Europe's major telecoms groups
major telecoms players
these companies
international telecoms groups
operators
the telecoms companies

the new technology
next generation of mobile phone technology
mobile data services
3G networks
3G technology
the new technology
mobile internet services
3G services

Vocabulary practice

1 INTERNAL PROCESSESS AND SYSTEMS
teleworking, electronic diary, hotdesking

RELATIONSHIPS WITH SUPPLIERS
vendor, extranet, supply chain management

RELATIONSHIPS WITH CUSTOMERS
e-commerce, personalised offerings, online billing,
telemarketing

2
2 personalise offerings
3 log onto the system
4 anticipate wants
5 simplify processes
6 download email

3
1 plan   4 schedule
2 duties   5 secure
3 configuration 6 optimise

Writing practice

1
1 repetition   3 wordiness / redundancy
2 reference words   4 redundancy / wordiness

2 See sample answer on page 76.

Unit 5: Human resources
Grammar practice

1
2 ... vacancies are going to be advertised?
3 ... vacancy has just been filled.
4 A new manager won't be recruited ...
5 Appraisal interveiws are normally held ...
6 All the applications haven't been processed ...
7 When were you interviewed?
8 ... jobs are being advertised ...

② 2 has been seriously affected
3 have been made
4 feel
5 are threatened
6 has been voiced
7 being placed
8 increase
9 have left / leave
10 have not been made
11 have been handled
12 will not be restored

③ 2 those   6 ones
3 the latter   7 such
4 the former   8 ones
5 this   9 these

Reading practice

① a) paragraph 3   e) paragraph 1
b) paragraph 4   f) paragraph 5
c) paragraph 2   g) paragraph 6
d) paragraph 7

② 1 Expanded too aggressively. Spent money more quickly than it generated profits.
2 Investors are doubting there is any money to be made from investing in online recruitment.
3 The market looks as if it will increase.
4 Advantages: jobhunters can search through thousands of vacancies and post CVs. Reduces company recruitment costs.
Disadvantages: cannot deal with sensitive hirings, security issues, saturated market.
5 Concentrate on its markets in Denmark, Germany and Belgium and try to raise finance.

③ 2 Monster   6 Elite
3 Elite   7 Channel 4
4 Channel 4, Stepstone   8 Ryanair
5 Stepstone

④

	six months ago	now
employees	876	351
share price	62 Kroner	0.3 Kroner
markets	UK, Denmark Belgium, Germany Norway	Denmark, Belgium, Germany Norway
cash	£30m	£14

⑤ 2 e   5 a
3 f   6 d
4 g   7 c

Vocabulary practice

① 1 behaviour   4 forces
2 criteria   5 candidate
3 appointee

② Order: e, b, h, d, f, i, g, a, j, c

③ in-   un-
informal   unethical
indiscreet   unsatisfactory
inappropriate   unco-operative
inflexible   unenthusiastic

2 co-operative   6 satisfactory
3 unenthusiastic   7 inflexible
4 informal   8 inappropriate
5 discreet   9 unethical

Writing practice

① 2 e   5 a
3 d   6 c
4 f

② See sample answer on page 77.

Unit 6: Culture

Grammar practice

① 2 working   9 to make
3 to do   10 not to have
4 to meet   11 having
5 to be   12 having
6 working   13 to know
7 to get   14 to leave
8 to work   15 being

② 2 Shall we / We could take our overseas guests ...
3 We must / 'll have to socialise with ...
4 Can we / Are we allowed to drink ...
5 We couldn't / weren't able to set up a ...
6 Could / May / Can I bring a colleague ...

③ 1 mustn't   5 'll
2 couldn't   6 don't have to
3 Shall   7 are you going to
4 might   8 May

Reading practice

① b) paragraph 1   e) paragraph 7
c) paragraph 6   f) paragraph 5
d) paragraph 4   g) paragraph 2

② 2 Employers have to consult workers' councils on major strategic decisions.
3 Sector associations agree industry-wide wage settlements with unions.
4 The government and unions both enforce labour market regulation that discourages companies from cutting jobs during economic downturns.

❸
1 Banker (German)
2 Worker (Anglo-American)
3 Company executive (German)
4 Manager / Union representative (German)
5 Worker (Anglo-American)
6 Company executive (Anglo-American)
7 Banker (German)
8 Company executive (Anglo-American)
9 Worker (Anglo-American)

❹
2	hostile	6	defend
3	threat	7	withstand
4	damage	8	foreign raiders
5	combat		

Vocabulary practice

❶ EMPLOYEE BELIEFS
basic values, cultural values, mindset, value systems

COMPANY INITIATIVES
policies, organisational hierarchy, positioning

PUBLIC DISPLAYS
products, dress code, uniform, status symbols

❷
2	optimism	5	humility
3	cost-conscious	6	validity
4	vitality		

❸
2	pretentious	5	rebuke
3	elite	6	symbol
4	diverse		

Writing practice

❶
1 F (Formality depends totally on the reader.)
2 F (Emails of introduction are very common.)
3 F (Length depends on content and reader.)
4 T (Very informal emails can be just a few words.)
5 T (Formality depends on the reader.)

❷ See sample answer on pages 77 and 78.

Unit 7: Ethics

Grammar practice

❶
2	e	5	d
3	f	6	a
4	c		

❷
2	bans	6	did
3	would go	7	carried
4	are	8	'd get
5	carried	9	would be

❸
2 offer, don't accept
3 wouldn't have blown, 'd been
4 harass, 'll get

5 wouldn't want, thought
6 wouldn't be, 'd issued
7 was / were caused, will / would face
8 will / would get, awards / awarded
9 wouldn't invest, found, were
10 wouldn't have been able, 'd had

Reading practice

❶
1	b	5	c
2	c	6	b
3	a	7	a
4	a	8	c

❷
2	a	7	c
3	j	8	f
4	d	9	h
5	i	10	g
6	e		

Vocabulary practice

❶
1	gossip	4	harassment
2	prejudice	5	perpetrator
3	privacy	6	mismanagement

❷
2	political correctness	6	information security
3	whistle-blower	7	shady practices
4	good causes	8	public sector
5	industrial espionage		

❸
2	e	5	a
3	f	6	d
4	c		

❹
2	hack into a system	6	bear a grudge
3	comply with the law	7	take legal action
4	commit a crime	8	pay a fine
5	issue passwords		

Writing practice

❶ See sample answer on page 78.

Unit 8: Globalisation

Grammar practice

❶
2 ... whether / if I had sent the brochures.
3 ... whether / if I was going to the trade ...
4 ... when I had arrived in Bahrain.
5 ... they were negotiating a deal with ...
6 ... they would dispatch the order the next day.

❷
2 ... warned Stone & Co not to contest the legal action.
3 ... refused to accept any charges of racial ...
4 ... recommended appointing / that the company appoint an ethics officer and draw up an official

code of ethics.

5 ... agreed that Mr Giddins had been dismissed according to the disciplinary code and that he had no grounds for unfair dismissal.

❸ 2 No sooner had we found a joint venture partner than they went bankrupt.
3 Little did I know that they were selling on the black market for $10 each.
4 We can reduce the features but on no account are we going to compromise on quality.
5 Never have I experienced such a dramatic rise and fall in a company's fortunes.
6 Only in markets where English is spoken can we sell our products.

Reading practice

❶ 2 Martina, Prague
3 Sourav, Mombai
4 John, Washington DC
5 Sourav, Mombai
6 John, Washington DC
7 Martina, Prague
8 John, Washington DC

❷ 1 International Monetary Fund (IMF) meeting in Seattle
2 Violent anti-globalisation protests
3 Anti-poverty campaigners, environmentalists, trade unions, human rights activists
4 One-day strike in India
5 Satellite TV, mass tourism and multinationals selling the same goods in every country
6 Because of its large semi-skilled workforce and strengths in information technology

❸

OPPORTUNITIES	THREATS
culture: Increased trade brings an increased understanding of other cultures.	**culture:** Reduction of cultural variety.
environment: Globalisation helps set higher environmental standards.	**environment:** Multinationals stronger than governments and not concerned with environmental sustainability.
governments: Globalisation spreads democracy and improves human rights.	**governments:** Not strong enough to make multinationals legally accountable.
products: Increased choice of products.	**products:** People will only be able to buy the same goods in every country.

OPPORTUNITIES	THREATS
film / television:	**film / television:** National film industries will die as all films are made in Hollywood.
mass tourism: Exposes people to other cultures and improves understanding of them.	**mass tourism:**

❹ 2 f 6 c
3 g 7 a
4 e 8 d
5 h

Vocabulary practice

❶ STRATEGIES
strategic alliance, buying the market, full ownership
RISKS
negative publicity, lower quality, cultural differences, currency exchange fluctuations
BENEFITS
lower labour costs, competitive advantage, global presence, access to markets, shorter time to market

❷ 2 of 6 in
3 with 7 to
4 up 8 into
5 for

❸ 2 e 5 d
3 a 6 c
4 f 7 g

Writing practice

❶ See sample answers on pages 79 and 80.

Review units

Review 1 (Units 1–4) Grammar

❶
1 do you want
2 're doing
3 have happened / have been happening
4 have held / have been holding / are holding
5 copied / 've copied
6 happened / has happened / has been happening
7 went
8 were / are
9 has ground
10 've been looking
11 might have found
12 have
13 're currently negotiating
14 is
15 Did you know
16 knew
17 happened
18 doesn't keep
19 have
20 don't know
21 don't think
22 've already taken
23 said
24 has had
25 agree

❷
1 who / that
2 which / that
3 which
4 whose
5 that / which
6 that / which / Ø
7 who / that
8 that / which
9 whose
10 which

❸
1 dramatically
2 original
3 suddenly
4 slightly
5 brief
6 stable
7 steadily
8 low
9 encouragingly
10 badly
11 reasonably
12 quick
13 steady
14 sharply
15 well

❹
1 'll reveal, make / 've made
2 'll cut, is
3 won't be able, approves / has approved
4 won't release, are taking
5 need / 'll need, receive
6 won't make, 've read
7 'll find, is falling
8 goes / has gone, 'll be
9 won't know, have / 've had
10 need, look

❺
1 the
2 a
3 an
4 Ø
5 the
6 Ø
7 Ø / the
8 an / Ø
9 a
10 the
11 the
12 a
13 Ø
14 the
15 Ø

❻
1 Are you going
2 will / is going to be
3 is it being held
4 Are you flying
5 leaves
6 'm not going to get
7 'm flying
8 are you doing
9 'm doing
10 'm also helping
11 are going to be
12 will / are going to be
13 'll / 're going to be
14 'll / 'm going to enjoy
15 won't be

❼
1 'll be arriving
2 'll be thinking
3 won't have finished
4 Will you be visiting
5 will have launched
6 won't be doing
7 won't have heard
8 won't be making
9 'll have lost
10 'll be looking

Review 1 (Units 1–4) Vocabulary

1 a) clarify
2 c) bandwagon
3 b) perceptions
4 c) diversify
5 a) rigid
6 b) commitment
7 a) initiate
8 c) intranet
9 c) operating
10 c) floating
11 a) integrate
12 b) an all-share
13 c) stand
14 b) mailshot
15 b) plummeted
16 a) download
17 c) radically
18 b) complexity
19 b) burst
20 a) anticipating
21 b) streamline
22 c) prestigious
23 b) independent
24 c) compatible
25 b) static
26 c) hampered
27 a) dividend
28 b) discourteous
29 b) agenda
30 a) specifications
31 c) break even
32 b) brochures
33 c) lease
34 a) arising
35 b) assets
36 c) retailers
37 c) hotdesking
38 a) collaboration
39 a) inflated
40 c) displays
41 c) obligations
42 b) allocated
43 b) schedule
44 c) sell-off
45 c) gifts
46 b) hierarchy
47 a) communication
48 c) equity stake
49 a) inventory
50 c) consolidation

Review 2 (Units 5–8) Grammar

❶
1 this
2 such
3 these / such
4 this / these
5 This
6 these / they

7 The former
8 the latter
9 these
10 this / that
11 the ones / those
12 This
13 this
14 the ones / those
15 this / it

2
1 seeing
2 to mention
3 to supply
4 to close
5 to meet
6 to accept
7 losing
8 risking
9 to produce
10 to increase
11 recruiting
12 to talk
13 to install
14 to man
15 Training
16 having
17 to train
18 researching
19 advertising
20 not to book

3
1 was carried
2 might be judged
3 was found
4 are sourced / were sourced
5 is employed
6 could be seen
7 have been published
8 are produced
9 are sold
10 are located
11 could easily be put
12 might also be affected
13 happened
14 to be taken
15 is recommended

4
1 b	5 a	9 c	13 b
2 b	6 b	10 a	14 a
3 a	7 b	11 c	15 c
4 c	8 c	12 b	

5
1 He admitted sending them the sales figures.
2 She suggested advertising on the internet.
3 He warned me not to use his office email address because his boss sometimes checked it.
4 She invited me to attend an interview on 23 October at 10 am.
5 He promised not to tell anyone that I was looking for a new job.
6 She asked whether I had any experience of working with html.
7 He denied lying on his CV.
8 She advised me to phone up and ask to speak to the HR Officer.
9 He reminded me to put some information about my hobbies on my CV.
10 She complained that there were too many applications and that she wouldn't be able to read them all before the next day.

6
1 don't look, 'll fall
2 hadn't lost, wouldn't have closed
3 wouldn't be, 'd secured
4 are, call
5 would be affecting / have affected, didn't have
6 were lost, 'll have
7 will call, goes
8 continue, 'll beat / 'll have beaten
9 wouldn't have licensed, hadn't been
10 Don't let, see / 've seen
11 'd found, would have pursued
12 'd adapt, were
13 are shipped, 'll arrive
14 had been signed, 'd all be making
15 didn't leave, 'll have arrived

7
1 ... had they completed the merger than they ...
2 ... can we accept the terms of the deal.
3 ... sign the contract until I get there.
4 ... before has the company made such profits.
5 ... that there would be a bomb scare ...
6 ... when you live in another country can you ...
7 ... do they not work late but they also don't work weekends either.
8 ... do you meet a British person who speaks ...
9 ... when / after the contract has been translated into French will we sign it.
10 ... should people be sent abroad without ...

Review 2 (Units 6–10) Vocabulary

1 b) satisfaction		26 a) initiatives
2 c) humility		27 b) devise
3 a) gift-giving		28 a) defective
4 c) alliance		29 b) search
5 a) retainer		30 c) optimistic
6 c) mission		31 c) compliance
7 b) urban legends		32 a) selection
8 c) hop		33 b) valid
9 c) appointee		34 b) whistle-blower
10 b) code		35 b) synonymous
11 c) infiltrated		36 a) issue
12 a) portrays		37 c) warning
13 b) criteria		38 c) implications
14 c) positioning		39 b) vendors
15 a) hacking		40 c) discreet
16 b) publicity		41 b) mindset
17 c) newsgroups		42 b) foul play
18 a) clones		43 a) time
19 c) harassment		44 a) niche
20 c) catalyst		45 c) thrift
21 a) rotation		46 c) principles
22 b) status symbols		47 b) correctness
23 c) gossip		48 a) prejudice
24 c) exchange risk		49 b) dilemmas
25 b) motivational		50 b) measures

Sample report: Unit 1, page 11

Report on improving project team communication

Introduction

The aim of this report is to identify communication problems within the new project team and recommend ways of improving this communication.

Findings

To begin with, individual interviews were held with all eight team members. Each team member also completed a questionnaire, which was designed to highlight the effectiveness of communication within the team. Several key issues arose from this feedback.

1) Although individual team members meet fairly frequently to discuss the project, the outcome of these discussions is not shared amongst other team members. Furthermore, these individual meetings are creating mini-teams within the team. This, of course, damages team spirit.

2) The eight team members are located in different parts of the building. This does not encourage contact and results in the situation outlined in Point 1.

3) Team members do not make enough effort to share information by email. Messages are sent to one person only and not copied to colleagues.

Conclusion

No evidence of personnel problems was found amongst team members. The lack of communication is due to difficulty with procedures and location, both of which should be easy to solve.

Recommendations

1) It is recommended that whole team meet on a weekly basis to share information and time together.

2) Team members should remember to copy colleagues in on emails relating to the project. This may require some training with the email software.

3) It has been suggested that the team attend a team-building seminar or adventure weekend. This would be a good idea.

Sample short report: Unit 2, page 17

In general, sales performed better in 2001 than in the previous year. Despite a three-month collapse in autumn, they finished the year higher than the previous year. Sales also fluctuated a lot more than in 2000.

Sales rose slowly in the first quarter, from $550,000 to $750,000, which was slightly down on the previous year. However, in May 2001 there was a sharp increase with sales peaking at $920,000, compared to less than $800,000 in 2000. Despite strong sales in June and July, both well up on 2000, there was a collapse from August to October with sales falling below $500,000. However, sales recovered in November and finished the year well, performing better than the previous year. December 2001 sales finished at $750,000, about $50,000 up on 2000.

Answer key

Key

75

Sample formal letter: Unit 3, page 23

Dear Mr van Rijn

Re: Futuresoft International 2003

I am writing <u>with reference to</u> your enquiry of 12 July. <u>We are pleased to confirm that</u> there are still display spots available for the Futuresoft International Exhibition 2003, which will be held at Earls Court, London on 24–26 October 2003.

<u>Please find enclosed</u> a floor plan showing the available spots along with a booking form. I have also enclosed information on display stand guidelines and the availability of power sources in the exhibition hall.

We recommend that you return the completed application form as soon as possible as all applications must be returned by 1 September. Could you please submit product information, samples and details of your proposed display stand along with your completed application form? Once you receive confirmation that your application has been accepted, full payment will be required by 1 October.

<u>Should you have any questions,</u> <u>please do not hesitate to</u> contact me on 0044 20 7632 7588.

Thank you for your interest in Futuresoft International. <u>We look forward to hearing from you</u> soon.

Yours sincerely

Sample short report: Unit 4, page 29

The graph shows the total UK sales per day of the week for Millennium Textiles' two best selling product lines – Ladies Office Wear and Ladies Casual Wear.

Beginning with Ladies Office Wear, nearly £90,000 worth of goods was sold on Mondays during the year 2001. This figure rose sharply to £130,000 for Tuesdays. Wednesdays and Thursdays were similar with sales of £140,000 and £135,000. There was a sharp rise in sales on Saturdays and Sundays, with total sales of £220,000 and £190,000 respectively.

Sales of Ladies Casual Wear were substantially lower Mondays to Fridays. Only £50,000 worth of Ladies Casual Wear was sold on Mondays in the year 2001, £40,000 less than Office Wear. The graph shows £60,000 for Tuesdays, £65,000 for Wednesdays, £72,000 for Thursdays and £68,000 for Fridays. Once again sales rose at weekends, with sales of £280,000 on Saturdays in 2001 and £275,000 on Sundays.

Sample formal report: Unit 5, page 41

Report on company staffing requirements

Introduction

The aim of this report is to consider current staffing levels and recommend whether more staff need to be recruited.

Findings

All heads of department were asked to consider staffing requirements and assess whether new employees were needed.

Due to recent reorganisation, the Sales Department urgently needs a new representative for the Mediterranean markets. The importance of the markets means we need to appoint a candidate with considerable experience.

The Production Department were concerned about holiday cover over the summer and the loss of staff through retirement later in the year. They would like to recruit five more workers.

The Secretarial Department would like two new employees to provide cover for maternity leave that may well be long-term.

Conclusion

It is clear that the Sales Department's need is greatest. Although both Production and Secretarial Departments need short-term cover, they have both asked for more staff than they are losing.

Recommendations

1) It is recommended that we start to recruit a new sales representative immediately by advertising in national newspapers and trade magazines.

2) Temporary positions should also be advertised in local newspapers for four production workers and one secretary. If the successful candidates prove reliable, they can be offered full-time contracts to replace employees retiring or not returning from maternity leave.

Sample email: Unit 6, page 47

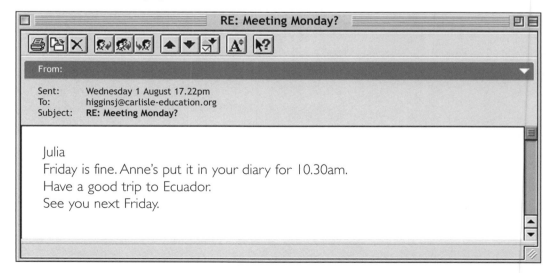

RE: Meeting Monday?

Sent: Wednesday 1 August 17.22pm
To: higginsj@carlisle-education.org
Subject: RE: Meeting Monday?

Julia
Friday is fine. Anne's put it in your diary for 10.30am.
Have a good trip to Ecuador.
See you next Friday.

Sample email: Unit 6, page 47 (continued)

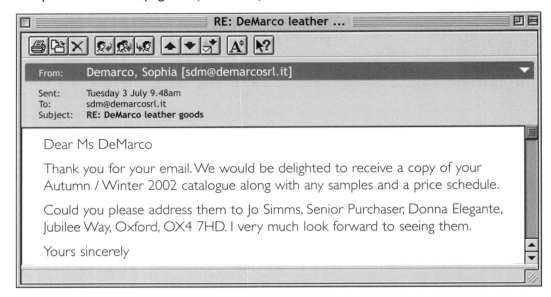

Dear Ms DeMarco

Thank you for your email. We would be delighted to receive a copy of your Autumn / Winter 2002 catalogue along with any samples and a price schedule.

Could you please address them to Jo Simms, Senior Purchaser, Donna Elegante, Jubilee Way, Oxford, OX4 7HD. I very much look forward to seeing them.

Yours sincerely

Sample report: Unit 7, page 53

Report on information security

Introduction

The aim of this report is to assess information security within the company and recommend ways of improving it.

Findings

Research has identified the following weaknesses in company security.

Firstly, all members of staff have access to all areas of the central database regardless of seniority. It is clear that access to sensitive information such as client lists should be restricted to those who genuinely need to use it.

Secondly, all staff computers are fitted with disk drives that allow files to be easily copied and taken from the building. As files can be exchanged internally using the network, there is no need for disk drives to be operational, except for when staff need to take work home.

Finally, staff do not use log-on codes to access the database so there is no record of who has accessed what information. Passwords would be a simple solution to this, despite the inconvenience of some staff forgetting them.

Conclusion

It is clear that the level of information security is very poor in the company. However, a few simple steps will greatly improve this.

Recommendations

Firstly, the company should grade all information in the database and restrict access according to rank and duties. In order to do this, the company needs to assign log-on codes and passwords to all staff. Finally, all disk drives should be disabled, except for those used by senior PAs. Anyone wishing to take files out of the building should only do so by requesting copies through these PAs.

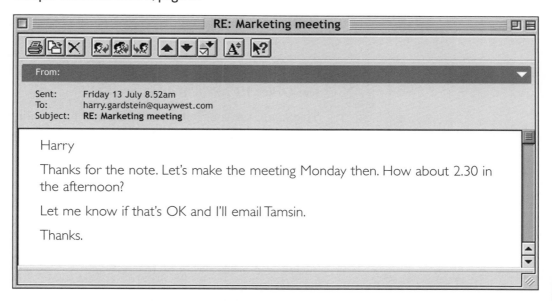

RE: Marketing meeting
From:
Sent: Friday 13 July 8.52am
To: harry.gardstein@quaywest.com
Subject: RE: Marketing meeting

Harry

Thanks for the note. Let's make the meeting Monday then. How about 2.30 in the afternoon?

Let me know if that's OK and I'll email Tamsin.

Thanks.

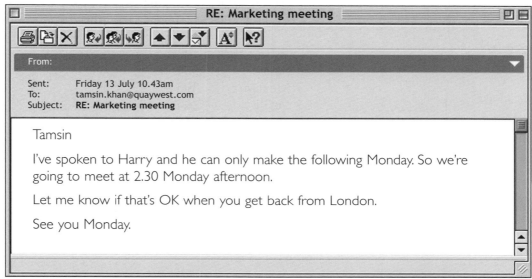

RE: Marketing meeting
From:
Sent: Friday 13 July 10.43am
To: tamsin.khan@quaywest.com
Subject: RE: Marketing meeting

Tamsin

I've spoken to Harry and he can only make the following Monday. So we're going to meet at 2.30 Monday afternoon.

Let me know if that's OK when you get back from London.

See you Monday.

May Production Report

Overall output in May rose steadily throughout the month and was ahead of the previous month's figures in each individual week. However, it must be noted that there were serious supply problems that affected production at the start of April.

May began slightly up on the last week of April with production at just under 80,000 units, which was over 10,000 units up month on month. This figure rose to about 85,000 units for the next two weeks, slightly ahead of April's peak of 82,000. Then, as the new machinery really began to take effect, output in the fourth week of May broke the 90,000 level to set a new weekly production record of 91,320 units. This figure was almost 14,000 units up on the same week in April.

Total output in May was almost 340,000 units, which was an increase of over 45,000 compared to April even taking April's problems into account, which was a great achievement.

Dear Mr Li

Re: Order RF20078/01

Thank you for your letter of 11 July and for bringing these matters concerning the order to our attention. Here are our wishes regarding the points you raised in your letter.

1) Article HX02/0240. Could you please change the order quantity to 300 pairs as suggested and amend the invoice to include the 3% discount. Thank you for pointing this out.

2) Article HX02/0081. Could you please cancel this item as we do not wish to order an alternative colour.

3) Article HX02/0009. I'm sorry I missed off the order quantities. Could you please produce the following quantities.

Extra Large	100
Large	300
Medium	300
Small	200

We would also like to confirm the delivery date as 1 March as agreed at our last meeting. Please accept our apologies for the incorrect date on the order form.

Should you have any other queries, please do not hesitate to contact me. Otherwise, we look forward to receiving the goods in March.

Yours sincerely